THE COMPLETE BOOK OF
BAKING

200 IRRESISTIBLE, EASY-TO-MAKE RECIPES FOR CAKES,
PIES, MUFFINS, TARTS, BUNS, BREADS AND COOKIES,
SHOWN STEP BY STEP IN OVER 850 PHOTOGRAPHS

CAROLE CLEMENTS

HERMES
HOUSE

This edition is published by Hermes House, an imprint of Anness Publishing Ltd,
Hermes House, 88–89 Blackfriars Road, London SE1 8HA; tel. 020 7401 2077; fax 020 7633 9499

www.hermeshouse.com; www.annesspublishing.com

If you like the images in this book and would like to investigate using them for publishing, promotions or
advertising, please visit our website www.practicalpictures.com for more information.

Publisher: Joanna Lorenz
Project editor: Carole Clements
Designer: Sheila Volpe
Photography, styling: Amanda Heywood
Food styling: Elizabeth Wolf-Cohen, Carla Capalbo
Steps: Cara Hobday, Teresa Goldfinch, Nicola Fowler

ETHICAL TRADING POLICY

At Anness Publishing we believe that business should be conducted in an ethical and ecologically sustainable way,
with respect for the environment and a proper regard to the replacement of the natural resources we employ.
As a publisher, we use a lot of wood pulp to make high-quality paper for printing, and that wood commonly comes from spruce trees.
We are therefore currently growing more than 750,000 trees in three Scottish forest plantations: Berrymoss (130 hectares/320 acres),
West Touxhill (125 hectares/305 acres) and Deveron Forest (75 hectares/185 acres). The forests we manage contain more than 3.5 times
the number of trees employed each year in making paper for the books we manufacture.
Because of this ongoing ecological investment programme, you, as our customer, can have the pleasure and reassurance of knowing
that a tree is being cultivated on your behalf to naturally replace the materials used to make the book you are holding.
Our forestry programme is run in accordance with the UK Woodland Assurance Scheme (UKWAS) and will be certified by the
internationally recognized Forest Stewardship Council (FSC). The FSC is a non-government organization dedicated to promoting
responsible management of the world's forests. Certification ensures forests are managed in an environmentally sustainable
and socially responsible way. For further information about this scheme, go to www.annesspublishing.com/trees

A CIP catalogue record for this book is available from the British Library.

Previously published as *Baking*

NOTES

Bracketed terms are intended for American readers.
For all recipes, quantities are given in both metric and imperial measures and, where appropriate, in standard cups and spoons.
Follow one set of measures, but not a mixture, because they are not interchangeable.
Standard spoon and cup measures are level. 1 tsp = 5ml, 1 tbsp = 15ml, 1 cup = 250ml/8fl oz.
Australian standard tablespoons are 20ml. Australian readers should use 3 tsp in place of 1 tbsp for measuring small quantities.
American pints are 16fl oz/2 cups. American readers should use 20fl oz/2.5 cups in place of 1 pint when measuring liquids.
Electric oven temperatures in this book are for conventional ovens. When using a fan oven, the temperature will probably need
to be reduced by about 10–20°C/20–40°F. Since ovens vary, you should check with your manufacturer's instruction book for guidance.
Medium (US large) eggs are used unless otherwise stated.

Main front cover image shows Orange and Raisin Scones – for recipe, see page 92

PUBLISHER'S NOTE

Although the advice and information in this book are believed to be accurate and true at the time of going to press, neither the authors nor
the publisher can accept any legal responsibility or liability for any errors or omissions that may be made nor for any inaccuracies nor for any
harm or injury that comes about from following instructions or advice in this book.

CONTENTS

INTRODUCTION

Nothing equals the satisfaction of home baking. No commercial cake mix or shop-bought biscuit can match one that is made from the best fresh ingredients with all the added enjoyment that baking at home provides – the enticing aromas that fill the house and stimulate appetites, the delicious straight-from-the-oven flavour, as well as the pride of having created such wonderful goodies yourself.

This book is filled with familiar favourites as well as many other lesser known recipes. Explore the wealth of biscuits, cookies, buns, tea breads, yeast breads, pies, tarts, and cakes within these pages. Even if you are a novice baker, the easy-to-follow and clear step-by-step photographs will help you achieve good results. For the more experienced home baker, this book will provide some new recipes to add to your repertoire.

Baking is an exact science and needs to be approached in an ordered way. First read through the recipe from beginning to end. Set out all the required ingredients before you begin. Medium eggs are assumed unless specified otherwise, and they should be at room temperature for best results. Sift the flour after you have measured it, and incorporate other dry ingredients as specified in the individual recipes. If you sift the flour from a fair height, it will have more chance to aerate and lighten.

When a recipe calls for folding one ingredient into another, it should be done in a way that incorporates as much air as possible into the mixture. Use either a large metal spoon or a long rubber or plastic scraper. Gently plunge the spoon or scraper deep into the centre of the mixture and, scooping up a large amount of the mixture, fold it over. Turn the bowl slightly so each scoop folds over another part of the mixture.

No two ovens are alike. Buy a reliable oven thermometer and test the temperature of your oven. When possible bake in the centre of the oven where the heat is more likely to be constant. If using a fan-assisted oven, follow the manufacturer's guidelines for baking. Good quality baking tins can improve your results, as they conduct heat more efficiently.

Practice, patience and enthusiasm are the keys to confident and successful baking. The recipes that follow will inspire you to start sifting flour, breaking eggs and stirring up all sorts of delectable homemade treats – all guaranteed to bring great satisfaction to both the baker and those lucky enough to enjoy the results.

BISCUITS, COOKIES & BARS

KEEP THE BISCUIT TIN FILLED WITH THIS WONDERFUL ARRAY OF BISCUITS, COOKIES AND BARS – SOME SOFT AND CHEWY, SOME CRUNCHY AND NUTTY, SOME RICH AND SINFUL, AND SOME PLAIN AND WHOLESOME. ALL ARE IRRESISTIBLE.

Farmhouse Cookies

Makes 18

115g/4oz/¹/₂ cup butter or margarine,
    at room temperature

90g/3¹/₂ oz/generous 1 cup light
    brown sugar

65g/2¹/₂ oz/¹/₄ cup crunchy peanut butter

1 egg

50g/2oz/¹/₂ cup plain (all-purpose) flour

2.5ml/¹/₂ tsp baking powder

2.5ml/¹/₂ tsp ground cinnamon

pinch of salt

175g/6oz/1¹/₂ cups muesli (granola)

50g/2oz/¹/₃ cup raisins

50g/2oz/¹/₂ cup chopped walnuts

1 Preheat the oven to 180°C/350°F/
Gas 4. Grease a baking sheet.

2 With an electric mixer, cream the
butter or margarine and sugar until
light and fluffy. Beat in the peanut
butter. Beat in the egg.

3 ▲ Sift the flour, baking powder,
cinnamon and salt over the peanut
butter mixture and stir to blend. Stir
in the muesli, raisins and walnuts.
Taste the mixture to see if it needs
more sugar, as muesli varies.

4 ▲ Drop rounded tablespoonfuls of
the mixture on to the prepared baking
sheet about 2.5cm/1in apart. Press
gently with the back of a spoon to
spread each mound into a circle.

5 Bake until lightly coloured, about
15 minutes. With a metal spatula,
transfer to a rack to cool. Store in
an airtight container.

Crunchy Oatmeal Cookies

MAKES 14

175g/6oz/³/₄ cup butter or margarine,
    at room temperature

175g/6oz/scant 1 cup caster
    (superfine) sugar

1 egg yolk

175g/6oz/1¹/₂ cups plain (all-purpose) flour

5ml/1 tsp bicarbonate of soda
    (baking soda)

2.5ml/¹/₂ tsp salt

50g/2oz/¹/₂ cup rolled oats

50g/2oz/¹/₂ cup small crunchy
    nugget cereal

~ VARIATION ~

For Nutty Oatmeal Cookies,
substitute an equal quantity of
chopped walnuts or pecan nuts for
the cereal, and prepare as described.

1 ▲ With an electric mixer, cream
the butter or margarine and sugar
together until light and fluffy. Mix in
the egg yolk.

2 Sift over the flour, bicarbonate of
soda and salt, then stir into the butter
mixture. Add the oats and cereal
and stir to blend. Chill for at least
20 minutes. Meanwhile, preheat the
oven to 190°C/375°F/Gas 5. Grease a
baking sheet.

3 ▼ Roll the mixture into balls.
Place them on the sheet and flatten
with the bottom of a floured glass.

4 Bake until golden, 10–12 minutes.
With a metal spatula, transfer to a
rack to cool completely. Store in an
airtight container.

Farmhouse Cookies (top), Crunchy Oatmeal Cookies

Oaty Coconut Cookies

MAKES 48

175g/6oz/1³/4 cups quick-cooking oats

75g/3oz/1 cup desiccated (dry unsweetened) coconut

225g/8oz/1 cup butter or margarine, at room temperature

115g/4oz/generous ¹/2 cup caster (superfine) sugar, plus 30ml/2 tbsp

50g/2oz/¹/4 cup soft dark brown sugar

2 eggs

60ml/4 tbsp milk

7.5ml/1¹/2 tsp vanilla extract

115g/4oz/1 cup plain (all-purpose) flour

2.5ml/¹/2 tsp bicarbonate of soda (baking soda)

2.5ml/¹/2 tsp salt

5ml/1 tsp ground cinnamon

1 Preheat the oven to 200°C/400°F/ Gas 6. Lightly grease two baking sheets.

2 ▲ Spread the oats and coconut on an ungreased baking sheet. Bake until golden brown, 8–10 minutes, stirring occasionally.

3 With an electric mixer, cream the butter or margarine and both sugars until light and fluffy. Beat in the eggs, one at a time, then the milk and vanilla. Sift over the dry ingredients and fold in. Stir in the oats and coconut.

4 ▼ Drop spoonfuls of the mixture 2.5–5cm/1–2in apart on the prepared sheets and flatten with the bottom of a greased glass dipped in sugar. Bake until golden, 8–10 minutes. Transfer to a rack to cool.

Crunchy Jumbles

MAKES 36

115g/4oz/¹/2 cup butter or margarine, at room temperature

225g/8oz/generous 1 cup caster (superfine) sugar

1 egg

5ml/1 tsp vanilla extract

150g/5oz/³/4 cup plain (all-purpose) flour

2.5ml/¹/2 tsp bicarbonate of soda (baking soda)

pinch of salt

50g/2oz crisped rice cereal

175g/6oz chocolate chips

~ **VARIATION** ~

For even crunchier biscuits, add 50g/2oz/¹/3 cup walnuts, coarsely chopped, with the cereal and chocolate chips.

1 Preheat the oven to 180°C/350°F/ Gas 4. Lightly grease two baking sheets.

2 ▲ With an electric mixer, cream the butter or margarine and sugar until light and fluffy. Beat in the egg and vanilla. Sift over the flour, bicarbonate of soda and salt and fold in carefully.

3 ▼ Add the cereal and chocolate chips. Stir to mix thoroughly.

4 Drop spoonfuls of the mixture 2.5–5cm/1–2in apart on the sheets. Bake until golden, 10–12 minutes. Transfer to a rack to cool.

Oaty Coconut Cookies (top), Crunchy Jumbles

Ginger Cookies

MAKES 36

225g/8oz/generous 1 cup caster (superfine) sugar

90g/3½oz/generous 1 cup soft light brown sugar

115g/4oz/½ cup butter, at room temperature

115g/4oz/½ cup margarine, at room temperature

1 egg

90ml/6 tbsp black treacle (molasses)

250g/9oz/2¼ cups plain (all-purpose) flour

10ml/2 tsp ground ginger

2.5ml/½ tsp freshly grated nutmeg

5ml/1 tsp ground cinnamon

10ml/2 tsp bicarbonate of soda (baking soda)

2.5ml/½ tsp salt

1 Preheat the oven to 170°C/325°F/ Gas 3. Line two or three baking sheets with baking parchment; grease lightly.

2 ▲ With an electric mixer, cream half the caster sugar, the brown sugar, butter and margarine until light and fluffy. Add the egg and continue beating to blend well. Add the treacle.

3 ▲ Sift the flour, spices and bicarbonate of soda three times, then stir into the butter mixture. Refrigerate for 30 minutes.

4 ▲ Place the remaining sugar in a shallow dish. Roll tablespoonfuls of the biscuit mixture into balls, then roll the balls in the sugar to coat.

5 Place the balls 5cm/2in apart on the prepared sheets and flatten slightly. Bake until golden around the edges but soft in the middle, 12–15 minutes. Leave to stand for 5 minutes before transferring to a rack to cool.

~ **VARIATION** ~

To make Gingerbread Men, increase the amount of flour by 25g/1oz/ ¼ cup. Roll out the mixture and cut out shapes with a special cutter. Decorate with icing, if you like.

Orange Cookies

MAKES 30

115g/4oz/$\frac{1}{2}$ cup butter, at room temperature
200g/7oz/1 cup caster (superfine) sugar
2 egg yolks
15ml/1 tbsp fresh orange juice
grated rind of 1 large orange
200g/7oz/scant 2 cups plain (all-purpose) flour
10g/$\frac{1}{4}$oz/1 tbsp cornflour (cornstarch)
2.5ml/$\frac{1}{2}$ tsp salt
5ml/1 tsp baking powder

1 ▲ With an electric mixer, cream the butter and sugar until light and fluffy. Add the yolks, orange juice and rind, and continue beating to blend. Set aside.

2 In another bowl, sift together the flour, cornflour, salt and baking powder. Add to the butter mixture and stir until it forms a dough.

3 ▲ Wrap the dough in baking parchment and chill for 2 hours.

4 Preheat the oven to 190°C/375°F/Gas 5. Grease two baking sheets.

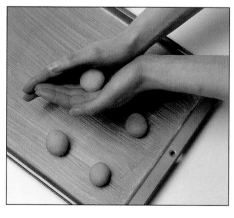

5 ▲ Roll spoonfuls of the dough into balls and place 2.5–5cm/1–2in apart on the prepared sheets.

6 ▼ Press down with a fork to flatten. Bake until golden brown, 8–10 minutes. With a metal spatula transfer to a rack to cool.

Cinnamon-coated Cookies

MAKES 30

115g/4oz/½ cup butter, at
room temperature

350g/12oz/1¾ cups caster
(superfine) sugar

5ml/1 tsp vanilla extract

2 eggs

50ml/2fl oz/¼ cup milk

400g/14oz/3½ cups plain (all-purpose) flour

5ml/1 tsp bicarbonate of soda
(baking soda)

50g/2oz/½ cup finely chopped walnuts

FOR THE COATING

65g/2½oz/5 tbsp sugar

30ml/2 tbsp ground cinnamon

1 Preheat the oven to 190°C/375°F/
Gas 5. Grease two baking sheets.

2 With an electric mixer, cream the butter until light. Add the sugar and vanilla and continue mixing until fluffy. Beat in the eggs, then the milk.

3 ▲ Sift the flour and bicarbonate of soda over the butter mixture and stir to blend. Stir in the nuts. Refrigerate for 15 minutes.

4 ▲ For the coating, mix the sugar and cinnamon. Roll tablespoonfuls of the mixture into walnut-size balls. Roll the balls in the sugar mixture. You may need to work in batches.

5 Place 5cm/2in apart on the prepared sheets and flatten slightly. Bake until golden, about 10 minutes. Transfer to a rack to cool.

Chewy Chocolate Cookies

MAKES 18

4 egg whites

275g/10oz/scant 2½ cups icing
(confectioners') sugar

115g/4oz/1 cup unsweetened cocoa powder

30ml/2 tbsp plain (all-purpose) flour

5ml/1 tsp instant coffee

15ml/1 tbsp water

115g/4oz/½ cup finely chopped walnuts

1 Preheat the oven to 180°C/350°F/
Gas 4. Line two baking sheets with baking parchment and grease the paper.

~ **VARIATION** ~

If wished, add 75g/3oz chocolate chips to the mixture with the nuts.

2 With an electric mixer, beat the egg whites until frothy.

3 ▼ Sift the sugar, cocoa, flour and coffee into the whites. Add the water and continue beating on low speed to blend, then on high for a few minutes until the mixture thickens. With a rubber spatula, fold in the walnuts.

4 ▲ Place generous spoonfuls of the mixture 2.5cm/1in apart on the prepared sheets. Bake until firm and cracked on top but soft on the inside, 12–15 minutes. With a metal spatula, transfer to a rack to cool.

Cinnamon-coated Cookies (top), Chewy Chocolate Cookies

Chocolate Pretzels

Makes 28

150g/5oz/1¼ cups plain
  (all-purpose) flour

pinch of salt

25g/¾oz/1 tbsp unsweetened cocoa powder

115g/4oz/½ cup butter, at
  room temperature

130g/4½oz/scant ¾ cup caster
  (superfine) sugar

1 egg

1 egg white, lightly beaten, for glazing

sugar crystals, for sprinkling

1 Sift together the flour, salt and cocoa powder. Set aside. Grease two baking sheets.

2 ▲ With an electric mixer, cream the butter until light. Add the sugar and continue beating until light and fluffy. Beat in the egg. Add the dry ingredients and stir to blend. Gather the dough into a ball, wrap in clear film (plastic wrap), and chill for 1 hour or freeze for 30 minutes.

3 ▲ Roll the dough into 28 small balls. Chill the balls until needed. Preheat the oven to 190°C/375°F/ Gas 5.

4 ▲ Roll each ball into a rope about 25cm/10in long. With each rope, form a loop with the two ends facing you. Twist the ends and fold back on to the circle, pressing in to make a pretzel shape. Place on the sheets.

5 ▲ Brush the pretzels with the egg white. Sprinkle sugar crystals over the tops and bake until firm, 10–12 minutes. Transfer to a rack to cool.

Cream Cheese Spirals

MAKES 32

225g/8oz/1 cup butter, at room temperature
225g/8oz/1 cup cream cheese
10ml/2 tsp caster (superfine) sugar
225g/8oz/2 cups plain (all-purpose) flour
1 egg white beaten with 15ml/1 tbsp water, for glazing
caster sugar, for sprinkling
FOR THE FILLING
115g/4oz/1 cup finely chopped walnuts
115g/4oz/½ cup soft light brown sugar
5ml/1 tsp ground cinnamon

1 With an electric mixer, cream the butter, cream cheese and sugar until soft. Sift over the flour and mix until combined. Gather into a ball and divide in half. Flatten each half, wrap in baking parchment and chill for at least 30 minutes.

2 Meanwhile, make the filling. Mix together the chopped walnuts, the brown sugar and the cinnamon, and set aside.

3 Preheat the oven to 190°C/375°F/ Gas 5. Grease two baking sheets.

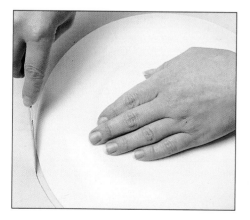

4 ▲ Working with one half of the mixture at a time, roll out thinly into a circle about 28cm/11in in diameter. Trim the edges with a knife, using a dinner plate as a guide.

5 ▼ Brush the surface with the egg white glaze and then sprinkle evenly with half the filling.

6 Cut the circle into quarters, and each quarter into four sections, to form 16 triangles.

7 ▲ Starting from the base of the triangles, roll up to form spirals.

8 Place on the sheets and brush with the remaining glaze. Sprinkle with caster sugar. Bake until golden, 15–20 minutes. Cool on a rack.

Vanilla Crescents

MAKES 36

175g/6oz/1 cup unblanched almonds

115g/4oz/1 cup plain (all-purpose) flour

pinch of salt

225g/8oz/1 cup unsalted (sweet) butter

115g/4oz/generous $^1/_2$ cup granulated sugar

5ml/1 tsp vanilla extract

icing (confectioners') sugar, for dusting

1 Grind the almonds with a few tablespoons of the flour in a food processor, blender or nut grinder.

2 Sift the remaining flour with the salt into a bowl. Set aside.

3 With an electric mixer, cream together the butter and sugar until light and fluffy.

4 ▼ Add the almonds, vanilla essence and the flour mixture. Stir to mix well. Gather the dough into a ball, wrap in baking parchment, and chill for at least 30 minutes.

5 Preheat the oven to 160°C/325°F/ Gas 3. Lightly grease two baking sheets.

6 ▲ Break off walnut-size pieces of dough and roll into small cylinders about 1cm/$^1/_2$in in diameter. Bend into small crescents and place on the prepared baking sheets.

7 Bake for about 20 minutes until dry but not brown. Transfer to a wire rack to cool only slightly. Set the rack over a baking sheet and dust with an even layer of icing sugar. Leave to cool completely.

Walnut Crescents

MAKES 9

115g/4oz/$^2/_3$ cup walnuts

225g/8oz/1 cup unsalted (sweet) butter

115g/4oz/generous $^1/_2$ cup granulated sugar

2.5ml/$^1/_2$ tsp vanilla extract

225g/8oz/2 cups plain (all-purpose) flour

1.5ml/$^1/_4$ tsp salt

icing (confectioners') sugar, for dusting

1 Preheat the oven to 180°C/350°F/ Gas 4.

2 Grind the walnuts in a food processor, blender or nut grinder until they are almost a paste. Transfer to a bowl.

3 Add the butter to the walnuts and mix with a wooden spoon until blended. Add the granulated sugar and vanilla, and stir to blend.

4 ▼ Sift the flour and salt into the walnut mixture. Work into a dough.

5 Shape the dough into small cylinders about 4cm/1$^1/_2$in long. Bend into crescents and place evenly spaced on an ungreased baking sheet.

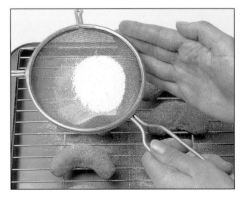

6 ▲ Bake until lightly browned, about 15 minutes. Transfer to a rack to cool only slightly. Set the rack over a baking sheet and dust lightly with icing sugar.

Vanilla Crescents (top), Walnut Crescents

Pecan Puffs

Makes 24

115g/4oz/¹/₂ cup unsalted (sweet) butter
25g/1oz/2 tbsp granulated sugar
pinch of salt
5ml/1 tsp vanilla extract
115g/4oz/²/₃ cup pecan nuts
115g/4oz/1 cup plain (all-purpose) flour, sifted
icing (confectioners') sugar, for dusting

1 Preheat the oven to 150°C/300°F/ Gas 2. Grease two baking sheets.

2 ▲ Cream the butter and sugar until light and fluffy. Stir in the salt and vanilla extract.

3 Grind the nuts in a food processor, blender or nut grinder. Stir several times to prevent them becoming oily. If necessary, grind in batches.

4 ▲ Push the ground nuts through a sieve (strainer) set over a bowl to aerate them. Pieces too large to go through the sieve can be ground again.

5 ▲ Stir the nuts and flour into the butter mixture to make a firm, springy dough.

6 Roll the dough into marble-size balls between the palms of your hands. Place on the prepared baking sheets and bake for 30 minutes.

7 ▲ While the puffs are still hot, roll them in icing sugar. Leave to cool completely, then roll once more in icing sugar.

Pecan Tassies

Makes 24

115g/4oz/^{1}/$_2$ cup cream cheese
115g/4oz/^{1}/$_2$ cup butter
115g/4oz/1 cup plain (all-purpose) flour
For the filling
2 eggs
115g/4oz/^{1}/$_2$ cup soft dark brown sugar
5ml/1 tsp vanilla extract
pinch of salt
25g/1oz/2 tbsp butter, melted
115g/4oz/^{2}/$_3$ cup pecan nuts

1 Place a baking sheet in the oven and preheat to 180°C/350°F/Gas 4. Grease 24 mini-muffin tins.

2 Chop the cream cheese and butter into cubes. Put them in a mixing bowl. Sift over half the flour and mix. Add the remaining flour and continue mixing to form a dough.

3 ▲ Roll out the dough thinly. With a floured, fluted pastry cutter, stamp out 24 6cm/2^1/$_2$in rounds. Line the tins with the rounds and chill.

> ### ~ VARIATION ~
> To make Jam Tassies, fill the cream cheese pastry shells with raspberry or blackberry jam, or other fruit jams. Bake as described.

4 To make the filling, lightly whisk the eggs in a bowl. Gradually whisk in the brown sugar, and add the vanilla extract, salt and butter. Set aside until required.

5 ▼ Reserve 24 undamaged pecan halves and chop the rest coarsely with a sharp knife.

6 ▲ Place a spoonful of chopped nuts in each muffin tin and cover with the filling. Set a pecan half on the top of each.

7 Bake on the hot baking sheet for about 20 minutes, until puffed and set. Transfer to a wire rack to cool. Serve at room temperature.

Lady Fingers

MAKES 18

90g/3¹/₂oz/³/₄ cup plain (all-purpose) flour

pinch of salt

4 eggs, separated

115g/4oz/generous ¹/₂ cup granulated sugar

2.5ml/¹/₂ tsp vanilla extract

icing (confectioners') sugar, for sprinkling

1 Preheat the oven to 150°C/300°F/ Gas 2. Grease two baking sheets, then coat lightly with flour, and shake off the excess.

2 Sift the flour and salt together twice in a bowl.

> **~ COOK'S TIP ~**
>
> To make the biscuits all the same length, mark parallel lines 10cm/4in apart on the greased baking sheets.

3 With an electric mixer beat the egg yolks with half the sugar until thick enough to leave a ribbon trail when the beaters are lifted.

4 ▲ In another bowl, beat the egg whites until stiff. Beat in the remaining sugar until glossy.

5 Sift the flour over the yolks and spoon a large dollop of egg whites over the flour. Carefully fold in with a large metal spoon, adding the vanilla extract. Gently fold in the remaining whites.

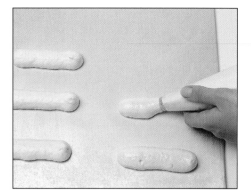

6 ▲ Spoon the mixture into a piping (pastry) bag fitted with a large plain nozzle. Pipe 10cm/4in long lines on the prepared baking sheets about 2.5cm/1in apart. Sift over a layer of icing sugar. Turn the sheet upside down to dislodge any excess sugar.

7 Bake for about 20 minutes until crusty on the outside but soft in the centre. Cool slightly on the baking sheets before transferring to a wire rack to cool completely.

Walnut Cookies

MAKES 60

115g/4oz/¹/₂ cup butter or margarine

175g/6oz/scant 1 cup caster (superfine) sugar

115g/4oz/1 cup plain (all-purpose) flour

10ml/2 tsp vanilla extract

115g/4oz/²/₃ cup walnuts, finely chopped

> **~ VARIATION ~**
>
> To make Almond Cookies, use an equal amount of finely chopped unblanched almonds instead of walnuts. Replace half the vanilla with 2.5ml/ ¹/₂ tsp almond essence.

1 Preheat the oven to 150°C/300°F/ Gas 2. Grease two baking sheets.

2 ▲ With an electric mixer, cream the butter or margarine until soft. Add 50g/2oz/¹/₄ cup of the sugar and continue beating until light and fluffy. Stir in the flour, vanilla extract and walnuts.

3 Drop teaspoonfuls of the batter 2.5–5cm/1–2in apart on the prepared baking sheets and flatten slightly. Bake for about 25 minutes.

4 ▼ Transfer to a wire rack set over a baking sheet and sprinkle with the remaining sugar.

Lady Fingers (top), Walnut Cookies

Italian Almond Biscotti

MAKES 48

200g/7oz/generous 1 cup whole unblanched almonds

215g/7¹/₂oz/scant 2 cups plain (all-purpose) flour

90g/3¹/₂oz/¹/₂ cup caster (superfine) sugar

pinch of salt

pinch of saffron threads

2.5ml/¹/₂ tsp bicarbonate of soda (baking soda)

2 eggs

1 egg white, lightly beaten

~ COOK'S TIP ~

Dunk biscotti in sweet white wine, such as an Italian Vin Santo or a French Muscat de Beaumes-de-Venise.

1 Preheat the oven to 190°C/375°F/ Gas 5. Grease and flour two baking sheets.

2 ▲ Spread the almonds in a baking tray and bake until lightly browned, about 15 minutes. When cool, grind 50g/2oz/¹/₃ cup of the almonds in a food processor, blender, or coffee grinder until pulverized. Coarsely chop the remaining almonds into two or three pieces each. Set aside.

3 ▲ Combine the flour, sugar, salt, saffron, bicarbonate of soda and ground almonds in a bowl and mix to blend. Make a well in the centre and add the eggs. Stir to form a rough dough. Transfer to a floured surface and knead until well blended. Knead in the chopped almonds.

4 ▲ Divide the dough into three equal parts. Roll into logs about 2.5cm/1in in diameter. Place on one of the prepared sheets, brush with the egg white and bake for 20 minutes. Remove from the oven.

5 ▲ With a very sharp knife, cut into each log at an angle making 1cm/ ¹/₂in slices. Return the slices on the baking sheets to a 140°C/275°F/Gas 1 oven and bake for 25 minutes more. Transfer to a rack to cool.

Christmas Cookies

MAKES 30

175g/6oz/³/₄ cup unsalted (sweet) butter, at room temperature

275g/10oz/scant 1¹/₂ cups caster (superfine) sugar

1 egg

1 egg yolk

5ml/1 tsp vanilla extract

grated rind of 1 lemon

1.5ml/¹/₄ tsp salt

275g/10oz/2¹/₂ cups plain (all-purpose) flour

FOR DECORATING (OPTIONAL)

coloured icing and small decorations

1 Preheat oven to 350°F/180°C/Gas 4.

2 ▲ With an electric mixer, cream the butter until soft. Add the sugar gradually and continue beating until light and fluffy.

3 ▲ Using a wooden spoon, slowly mix in the whole egg and the egg yolk. Add the vanilla, lemon rind and salt. Stir to mix well.

4 Add the flour and stir until blended. Gather the mixture into a ball, wrap in baking parchment, and chill for at least 30 minutes.

5 ▼ On a floured surface, roll out the mixture to 3mm/¹/₈in thick.

6 ▲ Stamp out shapes or rounds with biscuit (cookie) cutters.

7 Bake until lightly coloured, about 8 minutes. Transfer to a rack and leave to cool completely before icing and decorating, if wished.

Toasted Oat Meringues

MAKES 12

50g/2oz/¹/₂ cup rolled oats

2 egg whites

pinch of salt

7.5ml/1¹/₂ tsp cornflour (cornstarch)

175g/6oz/scant 1 cup caster (superfine) sugar

1 Preheat the oven to 140°C/275°F/Gas 1. Spread the oats on a baking sheet and toast in the oven until golden, about 10 minutes. Lower the heat to 120°C/250°F/Gas ¹/₂. Grease and flour a baking sheet.

> ~ **VARIATION** ~
>
> Add 2.5ml/¹/₂ tsp ground cinnamon with the oats, and fold in gently.

2 ▼ With an electric mixer, beat the egg whites and salt until they start to form soft peaks.

3 Sift over the cornflour and continue beating until the whites hold stiff peaks. Add half the sugar and whisk until glossy.

4 ▲ Add the remaining sugar and fold in, then fold in the oats.

5 Gently spoon the mixture on to the prepared sheet and bake for 2 hours.

6 When done, turn off the oven. Lift the meringues from the sheet, turn over, and set in another place on the sheet to prevent sticking. Leave in the oven as they cool down.

Meringues

MAKES 24

4 egg whites

pinch of salt

275g/10oz/scant 1¹/₂ cups caster (superfine) sugar

2.5ml/¹/₂ tsp vanilla or almond extract (optional)

250ml/8fl oz/1 cup whipped cream (optional)

1 Preheat the oven to 110°C/225°F/Gas ¹/₄. Grease and flour two large baking sheets.

2 With an electric mixer, beat the egg whites and salt in a very clean metal bowl on low speed. When they start to form soft peaks, add half the sugar and continue beating until the mixture holds stiff peaks.

3 ▲ With a large metal spoon, fold in the remaining sugar and vanilla or almond extract, if using.

4 ▼ Pipe the meringue mixture or spoon it on to the prepared sheet.

5 Bake for 2 hours. Turn off the oven. Loosen the meringues, invert, and set in another place on the sheets to prevent sticking. Leave in the oven as they cool. Serve sandwiched with whipped cream, if you wish.

Toasted Oat Meringues (top), Meringues

Chocolate Macaroons

MAKES 24

50g/2oz plain (semisweet) chocolate

175g/6oz/1 cup blanched almonds

225g/8oz/generous 1 cup caster (superfine) sugar

3 egg whites

2.5ml/¹/₂ tsp vanilla extract

1.5ml/¹/₄ tsp almond extract

icing (confectioners') sugar, for dusting

1 Preheat the oven to 300°F/150°C/ Gas 2. Line two baking sheets with baking parchment and grease the paper.

2 ▼ Melt the chocolate in the top of a double boiler, or in a heatproof bowl set over a pan of hot water.

3 ▲ Grind the almonds finely in a food processor, blender or grinder. Transfer to a mixing bowl.

4 ▲ In a mixing bowl, whisk the egg whites until they form soft peaks. Fold in the sugar, vanilla and almond extracts, ground almonds and cooled melted chocolate Chill for 15 minutes.

5 ▲ Use a teaspoon and your hands to shape the mixture into walnut-size balls. Place on the sheets and flatten slightly. Brush each ball with a little water and sift over a thin layer of icing sugar. Bake until just firm, 20–25 minutes. With a metal spatula, transfer to a rack to cool.

> ### ~ VARIATION ~
> For Chocolate Pine Nut Macaroons, spread 75g/3oz/³/₄ cup pine nuts in a shallow dish. Press the chocolate macaroon balls into the nuts to cover one side and bake as described, nut-side up.

Coconut Macaroons

MAKES 24

40g/1¹/₂oz/¹/₃ cup plain (all-purpose) flour

pinch of salt

225g/8oz/scant 3 cups desiccated (dry unsweetened) coconut

175ml/6fl oz/³/₄ cup sweetened condensed milk

5ml/1 tsp vanilla extract

1 Preheat the oven to 180°C/350°F/ Gas 4. Grease two baking sheets.

2 Sift the flour and salt into a bowl. Stir in the coconut.

3 ▲ Pour in the milk. Add the vanilla and stir from the centre to make a very thick mixture.

4 Drop heaped tablespoonfuls of mixture 2.5cm/1in apart on the sheets. Bake until golden brown, about 20 minutes. Cool on a rack.

Chocolate Macaroons (top), Coconut Macaroons

Almond Tuiles

MAKES 40

50g/2oz/^{1}/$_{3}$ cup blanched almonds
115g/4oz/generous ^{1}/$_{2}$ cup caster (superfine) sugar
50g/2oz/^{1}/$_{4}$ cup unsalted (sweet) butter
2 egg whites
40g/1^{1}/$_{2}$oz/^{1}/$_{3}$ cup plain (all-purpose) flour
2.5ml/^{1}/$_{2}$ tsp vanilla extract
115g/4oz/1 cup flaked (sliced) almonds

1 Grind the blanched almonds with 30ml/2 tbsp of the sugar in a food processor, blender or nut grinder. If necessary, grind in batches.

2 Preheat the oven to 220°C/425°F/ Gas 7. Grease two baking sheets.

3 ▲ Put the butter in a large bowl and mix in the remaining sugar, using a metal spoon. With an electric mixer, cream them together until light and fluffy.

4 Add the egg whites and stir until blended. Sift over the flour and fold in with a metal spoon. Fold in the ground almonds and vanilla extract.

5 ▲ Working in small batches, drop tablespoonfuls of the mixture 7.5cm/3in apart on one of the prepared sheets. With the back of a spoon, spread out into thin, almost transparent circles about 6cm/2^{1}/$_{2}$in in diameter. Sprinkle each circle with some of the flaked almonds.

6 Bake until the outer edges have browned slightly, about 4 minutes.

7 ▲ Remove from the oven. With a metal spatula, quickly drape the biscuits over a rolling pin to form a curved shape. Transfer to a rack when firm. If the biscuits harden too quickly to shape, reheat them briefly. Repeat the baking and shaping process until the mixture is used up. Store in an airtight container.

Florentines

MAKES 36

40g/1¹/₂oz/3 tbsp butter

120ml/4fl oz/¹/₂ cup whipping cream

130g/4¹/₂oz/scant ³/₄ cup caster (superfine) sugar

130g/4¹/₂oz/generous 1 cup flaked (sliced) almonds

50g/2oz/¹/₃ cup orange or mixed (candied) peel, finely chopped

40g/1¹/₂oz/¹/₄ cup glacé (candied) cherries, chopped

65g/2¹/₂oz/9 tbsp plain (all-purpose) flour, sifted

225g/8oz plain (semisweet) chocolate

5ml/1 tsp vegetable oil

1 ▲ Preheat the oven to 180°C/ 350°F/Gas 4. Grease two baking sheets. Melt the butter, cream and sugar together and slowly bring to the boil. Take off the heat and stir in the almonds, orange or mixed peel, cherries and flour until blended.

3 Drop teaspoonfuls of the batter 2.5–5cm/1–2in apart on the prepared sheets and flatten with a fork.

4 Bake for about 10 minutes until brown at the edges. Remove from the oven and correct the shape whilst they are hot by quickly pushing in any uneven edges with a knife or a round biscuit (cookie) cutter. If necessary, return to the oven for a few moments to soften. While still hot, use a metal spatula to transfer the florentines to a clean, flat surface.

5 Melt the chocolate in the top of a double boiler or in a heatproof bowl set over a pan of hot water. Add the oil and stir to blend.

6 ▲ With a palette knife (metal spatula), spread the smooth underside of the cooled florentines with a thin coating of the melted chocolate.

7 ▼ When the chocolate is about to set, draw a serrated knife across the surface with a slight sawing motion to make wavy lines. Store in an airtight container in a cool place.

Nut Lace Wafers

MAKES 18

65g/2¹/₂oz/¹/₂ cup whole blanched almonds

50g/2oz/¹/₄ cup butter

40g/1¹/₂oz/¹/₃ cup plain (all-purpose) flour

90g/3¹/₂oz/¹/₂ cup caster (superfine) sugar

30ml/2 tbsp double (heavy) cream

2.5ml/¹/₂ tsp vanilla extract

1 Preheat the oven to 190°C/375°F/ Gas 5. Grease one or two baking sheets.

2 With a sharp knife, chop the almonds as finely as possible. Alternatively, use a food processor, blender, or coffee grinder to chop the nuts very finely.

3 ▼ Melt the butter in a pan over low heat. Remove from the heat and stir in the remaining ingredients and the almonds.

4 Drop teaspoonfuls 6cm/2¹/₂in apart on the prepared sheets. Bake until golden, about 5 minutes. Cool on the baking sheets briefly, just until the wafers are stiff enough to remove.

5 ▲ With a palette knife (metal spatula), transfer to a rack to cool completely.

~ **VARIATION** ~

Add 50g/2oz finely chopped orange peel to the mixture.

Oatmeal Lace Rounds

MAKES 36

165g/5¹/₂oz/11 tbsp butter or margarine

130g/4¹/₂oz/1¹/₄ cups quick-cooking rolled oats

175g/6oz/scant 1 cup soft dark brown sugar

150g/5oz/³/₄ cup caster (superfine) sugar

40g/1¹/₂oz/¹/₃ cup plain (all-purpose) flour

1.5ml/¹/₄ tsp salt

1 egg, lightly beaten

5ml/1 tsp vanilla extract

65g/2¹/₂oz/¹/₂ cup pecan nuts or walnuts, finely chopped

1 Preheat the oven to 180°C/350°F/ Gas 4. Grease two baking sheets.

2 Melt the butter in a pan over low heat. Set aside.

3 In a mixing bowl, combine the oats, brown sugar, caster sugar, flour and salt.

4 ▲ Make a well in the centre and add the butter or margarine, egg and vanilla.

5 ▼ Mix until blended, then stir in the chopped nuts.

6 Drop rounded teaspoonfuls of the mixture about 5cm/2in apart on the prepared sheets. Bake until lightly browned on the edges and bubbling, 5–8 minutes. Leave to cool on the sheet for 2 minutes, then transfer to a rack to cool completely.

Nut Lace Wafers (top), Oatmeal Lace Rounds

Raspberry Sandwich Cookies

MAKES 32

175g/6oz/1 cup blanched almonds

175g/6oz/1½ cups plain (all-purpose) flour

175g/6oz/¾ cup butter, at room temperature

115g/4oz/generous ½ cup caster (superfine) sugar

grated rind of 1 lemon

5ml/1 tsp vanilla extract

1 egg white

pinch of salt

25g/1oz/¼ cup flaked (sliced) almonds

250ml/8fl oz/1 cup raspberry jam

15ml/1 tbsp fresh lemon juice

1 Place the blanched almonds and 20g/¾oz/3 tbsp of the flour in a food processor, blender or coffee grinder and process until finely ground. Set aside.

2 With an electric mixer, cream the butter and sugar together until light and fluffy. Stir in the lemon rind and vanilla. Add the ground almonds and remaining flour, and mix well until combined. Gather into a ball, wrap in baking parchment, and chill for at least 1 hour.

3 Preheat the oven to 160°C/325°F/ Gas 3. Line two baking sheets with baking parchment.

4 Divide the cookie mixture into four equal parts. Working with one section at a time, roll out to a thickness of 3mm/⅛in on a lightly floured surface. With a 6cm/2½in fluted pastry (cookie) cutter, stamp out circles. Gather the scraps, roll out and stamp out more circles. Repeat with the remaining sections.

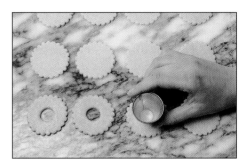

5 ▲ Using a 2cm/¾in piping nozzle or pastry cutter, stamp out the centres from half the circles. Place the rings and circles 2.5cm/1in apart on the prepared sheets.

6 ▲ Whisk the egg white with the salt until just frothy. Chop the flaked almonds. Brush only the biscuit rings with the egg white, then sprinkle over the almonds. Bake until very lightly browned, 12–15 minutes. Let cool for a few minutes on the sheets before transferring to a rack.

7 ▲ In a pan, melt the jam with the lemon juice until it comes to a simmer. Brush the jam over the biscuit circles and sandwich together with the rings. Store in an airtight container with sheets of baking parchment between the layers.

Brandysnaps

MAKES 18

50g/2oz/¹/₄ cup butter, at room temperature

150g/5oz/³/₄ cup caster (superfine) sugar

15ml/1 tbsp golden (light corn) syrup

40g/1¹/₂oz/¹/₃ cup plain (all-purpose) flour

2.5ml/¹/₂ tsp ground ginger

FOR THE FILLING

250ml/8fl oz/1 cup whipping cream

30ml/2 tbsp brandy

1 With an electric mixer, cream together the butter and sugar until light and fluffy, then beat in the golden syrup. Sift over the flour and ginger and mix together.

2 ▲ Transfer the mixture to a work surface and knead until smooth. Cover and chill for 30 minutes.

3 Preheat the oven to 190°C/375°F/ Gas 5. Grease a baking sheet.

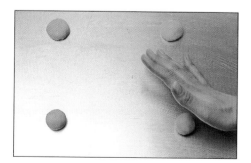

4 ▲ Working in batches of four, form the mixture into walnut-size balls. Place far apart on the sheet and flatten slightly. Bake until golden and bubbling, about 10 minutes.

5 ▼ Remove from the oven and let cool a few moments. Working quickly, slide a metal spatula under each one, turn over, and wrap around the handle of a wooden spoon (have four spoons ready). If they firm up too quickly, reheat for a few seconds to soften. When firm, slide the snaps off and place on a rack to cool.

6 ▲ When all the brandy snaps are cool, prepare the filling. Whip the cream and brandy until soft peaks form. Fill a piping (pastry) bag with the brandy cream. Pipe into each end of the brandy snaps just before serving.

Shortbread

MAKES 8

165g/5¹/₂oz/11 tbsp unsalted (sweet) butter, at room temperature

90g/3¹/₂oz/¹/₂ cup caster (superfine) sugar

185g/6¹/₂oz/1²/₃ cups plain (all-purpose) flour

50g/2oz/¹/₂ cup rice flour

1.5ml/¹/₄ tsp baking powder

pinch of salt

1 Preheat the oven to 170°C/325°F/ Gas 3. Grease a shallow 20cm/8in cake tin (pan), preferably with a removable base.

2 With an electric mixer, cream the butter and sugar together until light and fluffy. Sift over the flours, baking powder and salt, and mix well.

3 ▲ Press the dough neatly into the prepared tin, smoothing the surface with the back of a spoon.

4 Prick all over with a fork, then score into eight equal wedges.

5 ▲ Bake until golden, 40–45 minutes. Leave in the tin until cool enough to handle, then turn out and recut the wedges while still hot. Store in an airtight container.

Flapjacks

MAKES 8

50g/2oz/¹/₄ cup butter

15ml/1 tbsp golden (light corn) syrup

75g/3oz/¹/₃ cup soft dark brown sugar

90g/3¹/₂oz/1 cup quick-cooking rolled oats

pinch of salt

1 ▲ Preheat the oven to 180°C/ 350°F/Gas 4. Line a 20cm/8in cake tin with baking parchment and grease.

2 ▼ Place the butter, golden syrup and sugar in a pan over a low heat. Cook, stirring, until melted and combined.

~ **VARIATION** ~

If you like, add 5ml/1 tsp ground ginger to the melted butter.

3 ▲ Remove from the heat and add the oats and salt. Stir to blend.

4 Spoon into the prepared tin and smooth the surface. Place in the centre of the oven and bake until golden brown, 20–25 minutes. Leave in the tin until cool enough to handle, then turn out and cut into wedges while still hot.

Shortbread (top), Flapjacks

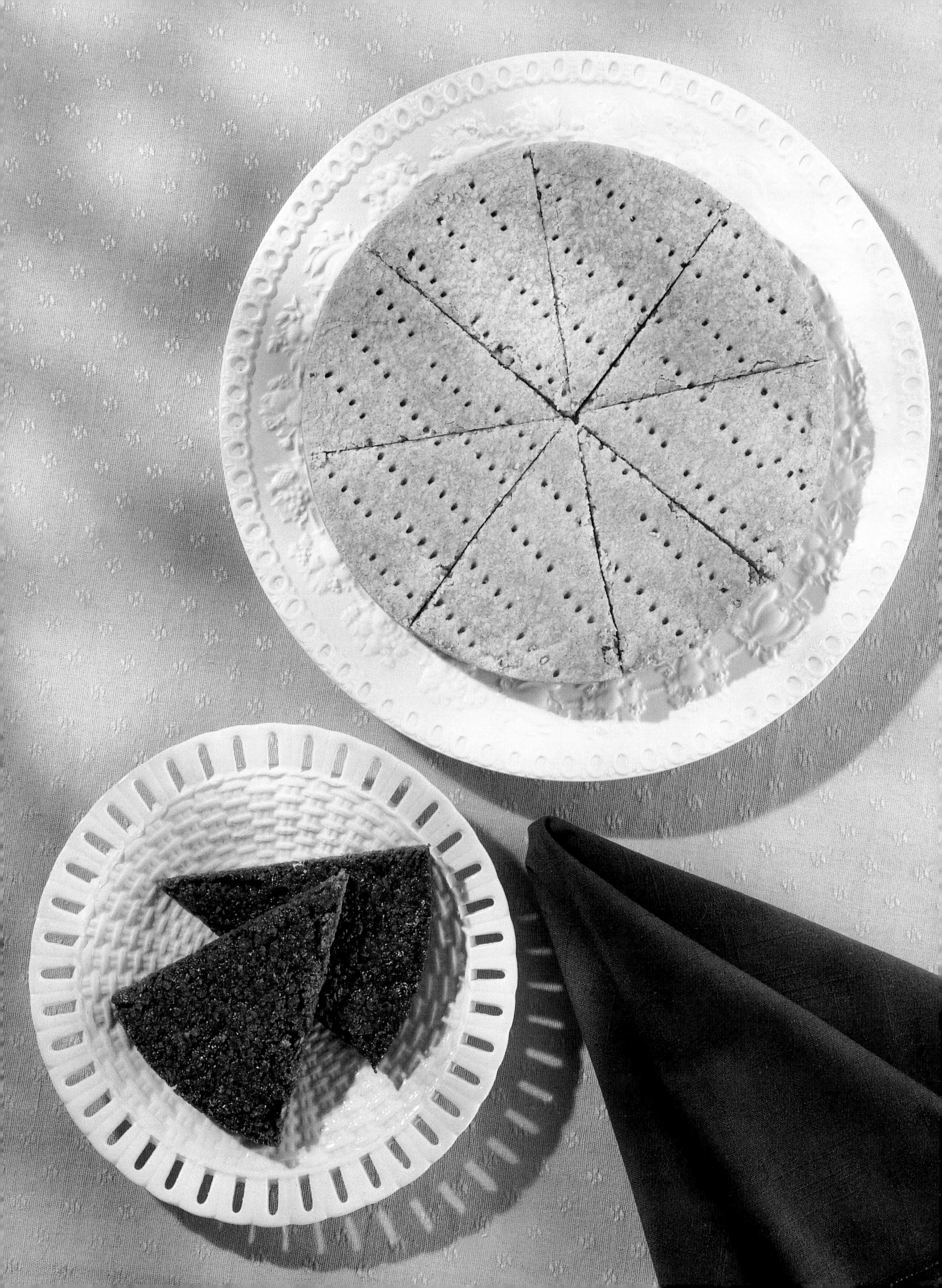

Chocolate Delights

MAKES 50

25g/1oz plain (semisweet) chocolate

25g/1oz dark (bittersweet)
  cooking chocolate

225g/8oz/2 cups plain (all-purpose) flour

2.5ml/¹⁄₂ tsp salt

225g/8oz/1cup unsalted (sweet) butter,
  at room temperature

225g/8oz/generous 1 cup caster
  (superfine) sugar

2 eggs

5ml/1 tsp vanilla extract

115g/4oz/1 cup finely chopped walnuts

1 Melt the chocolates in the top of a
double boiler, or in a heatproof bowl
set over a pan of gently simmering
water. Set aside.

2 ▼ In a small bowl, sift together the
flour and salt. Set aside.

3 With an electric mixer, cream the
butter until soft. Add the sugar and
continue beating until the mixture is
light and fluffy.

4 Mix the eggs and vanilla, then
gradually stir into the butter mixture.

5 ▲ Stir in the chocolate, then the
flour. Stir in the nuts.

6 ▲ Divide the mixture into four
equal parts, and roll each into 5cm/
2in diameter logs. Wrap tightly in foil
and refrigerate or freeze until firm.

7 Preheat the oven to 190°C/375°F/
Gas 5. Grease two baking sheets.

8 With a sharp knife, cut the logs
into 5mm/¹⁄₄in slices. Place the rounds
on the prepared sheets and bake until
lightly coloured, about 10 minutes.
Transfer to a rack to cool.

> ~ **VARIATION** ~
>
> For two-tone biscuits, melt only
> half the chocolate. Combine all
> the ingredients, except the
> chocolate, as above. Divide the
> mixture in half. Add the chocolate
> to one half. Roll out the plain
> mixture on to a flat sheet. Roll out
> the chocolate mixture, place on
> top of the plain one and roll up.
> Wrap, slice and bake as described.

Cinnamon Treats

MAKES 50

250g/9oz/2¼ cups plain (all-purpose) flour

2.5ml/½ tsp salt

10ml/2 tsp ground cinnamon

225g/8oz/1 cup unsalted (sweet) butter, at room temperature

225g/8oz/generous 1 cup caster (superfine) sugar

2 eggs

5ml/1 tsp vanilla extract

1 In a bowl, sift together the flour, salt and cinnamon. Set aside.

2 ▲ With an electric mixer, cream the butter until soft. Add the sugar and continue beating until the mixture is light and fluffy.

3 Beat the eggs and vanilla, then gradually stir into the butter mixture.

4 ▲ Stir in the dry ingredients.

5 ▲ Divide the mixture into four equal parts, then roll each into 5cm/2in diameter logs. Wrap tightly in foil and chill or freeze until firm.

6 Preheat the oven to 190°C/375°F/Gas 5. Grease two baking sheets.

7 ▼ With a sharp knife, cut the logs into 5mm/¼in slices. Place the rounds on the prepared sheets and bake until lightly coloured, about 10 minutes. With a metal spatula, transfer to a rack to cool.

Peanut Butter Cookies

MAKES 24

150g/5oz/1¼ cups plain
(all-purpose) flour

2.5ml/½ tsp bicarbonate of soda
(baking soda)

2.5ml/½ tsp salt

115g/4oz/½ cup butter,
at room temperature

165g/5½oz/¾ cup soft light brown sugar

1 egg

5ml/1 tsp vanilla extract

265g/9½oz/1¼ cups crunchy peanut
butter

1 Sift together the flour, bicarbonate of soda and salt, and set aside.

2 With an electric mixer, cream the butter and sugar together until light and fluffy.

3 In another bowl, mix together the egg and vanilla, then gradually beat into the butter mixture.

4 ▲ Stir in the peanut butter and blend thoroughly. Stir in the dry ingredients. Chill for at least 30 minutes, or until firm.

5 Preheat the oven to 180°C/350°F/ Gas 4. Grease two baking sheets.

6 Spoon out rounded teaspoonfuls of the dough and roll into balls.

7 ▲ Place the balls on the prepared sheets and press flat with a fork into circles about 6cm/2½in in diameter, making a criss-cross pattern. Bake until lightly coloured, 12–15 minutes. Transfer to a rack to cool.

```
~ VARIATION ~
Add 75g/3oz/½ cup peanuts, coarsely
chopped, with the peanut butter.
```

Chocolate Chip Cookies

MAKES 24

115g/4oz/½ cup butter or margarine,
at room temperature

50g/2oz/¼ cup caster (superfine) sugar

90g/3½oz/scant ½ cup soft dark
brown sugar

1 egg

2.5ml/½ tsp vanilla extract

175g/6oz/1½ cups plain (all-purpose) flour

2.5ml/½ tsp bicarbonate of soda
(baking soda)

pinch of salt

175g/6oz chocolate chips

50g/2oz/⅓ cup walnuts, chopped

1 Preheat the oven to 180°C/350°F/ Gas 4. Grease two large baking sheets.

2 ▼ With an electric mixer, cream the butter or margarine and two sugars together until light and fluffy.

3 In another bowl, mix the egg and vanilla, then gradually beat into the butter mixture. Sift over the flour, bicarbonate of soda and salt, and stir.

4 ▲ Add the chocolate chips and walnuts, and mix to combine well.

5 Place heaped teaspoonfuls of the dough 5cm/2in apart on the prepared sheets. Bake until lightly coloured, 10–15 minutes. Transfer to a rack to cool.

Peanut Butter Cookies (top), Chocolate Chip Cookies

Salted Peanut Cookies

Makes 70

350g/12oz/3 cups plain (all-purpose) flour

2.5ml/½ tsp bicarbonate of soda (baking soda)

115g/4oz/½ cup butter

115g/4oz/½ cup margarine

250g/9oz/generous 1 cup soft light brown sugar

2 eggs

10ml/2 tsp vanilla extract

225g/8oz/1⅓ cups salted peanuts

1 Preheat the oven to 190°C/375°F/ Gas 5. Lightly grease two baking sheets. Grease the bottom of a glass and dip in sugar.

2 Sift together the flour and bicarbonate of soda. Set aside.

3 ▲ Cream the butter, margarine and sugar. Beat in the eggs and vanilla extract. Fold in the flour mixture.

4 ▲ Stir the peanuts into the butter mixture until evenly combined.

5 ▲ Drop teaspoonfuls 5cm/2in apart on the prepared sheets. Flatten with the prepared glass.

6 Bake for about 10 minutes, until lightly coloured. With a metal spatula, transfer to a wire rack to cool.

~ **VARIATION** ~

To make Cashew Cookies, substitute an equal amount of salted cashew nuts for the peanuts, and add as above.

Cheddar Pennies

Makes 20

50g/2oz/¼ cup butter

115g/4oz/1⅓ cups Cheddar cheese, grated

40g/1½oz/⅓ cup plain (all-purpose) flour

pinch of salt

pinch of chilli powder

1 Put the butter in a large bowl and cut into 2.5cm/1in cubes. With an electric mixer, cream the butter until soft and fluffy.

2 ▲ Stir in the cheese, flour, salt and chilli. Gather to form a dough.

3 Transfer to a lightly floured surface. Shape into a cylinder about 3cm/ 1¼in in diameter. Wrap in baking parchment and chill for 1–2 hours.

4 Preheat the oven to 180°C/350°F/ Gas 4. Grease one or two baking sheets.

5 ▲ Cut the dough into 5mm/¼in thick slices and place on the prepared baking sheets. Bake for about 15 minutes, until golden. Transfer to a wire rack to cool.

Salted Peanut Cookies (top), Cheddar Pennies

Chocolate Chip Brownies

MAKES 24

115g/4oz plain (semisweet) chocolate

115g/4oz/¹/₂ cup butter

3 eggs

200g/7oz/1 cup caster (superfine) sugar

2.5ml/¹/₂ tsp vanilla extract

pinch of salt

150g/5oz/1¹/₄ cups plain (all-purpose) flour

175g/6oz chocolate chips

1 ▼ Preheat the oven to 180°C/350°F/ Gas 4. Line a 33 × 23cm/13 × 9in tin (pan) with baking parchment and grease.

2 ▲ Melt the chocolate and butter in the top of a double boiler, or in a heatproof bowl set over a pan of gently simmering water.

3 ▲ Beat together the eggs, sugar, vanilla and salt. Stir in the chocolate mixture. Sift over the flour and fold in. Add the chocolate chips.

4 ▲ Pour the mixture into the prepared tin and spread evenly. Bake until just set, about 30 minutes. Do not overbake; the brownies should be slightly moist inside. Cool in the pan.

5 To turn out, run a knife all around the edge and invert on to a baking sheet. Remove the paper. Place another sheet on top and invert again so the brownies are right-side up. Cut into squares for serving.

Marbled Brownies

MAKES 24

225g/8oz plain (semisweet) chocolate
75g/3oz/6 tbsp butter
4 eggs
300g/11oz/generous 1½ cups caster (superfine) sugar
150g/5oz/1¼ cups plain (all-purpose) flour
2.5ml/½ tsp salt
5ml/1 tsp baking powder
10ml/2 tsp vanilla extract
115g/4oz/⅔ cups walnuts, chopped
FOR THE PLAIN MIXTURE
50g/2oz/¼ cup butter, at room temperature
175g/6oz/¾ cup cream cheese
90g/3½oz/½ cup caster (superfine) sugar
2 eggs
25g/1oz/¼ cup plain (all-purpose) flour
5ml/1 tsp vanilla extract

1 Preheat the oven to 180°C/350°F/ Gas 4. Line a 33 × 23cm/13 × 9in tin (pan) with baking parchment and grease.

2 Melt the chocolate and butter over very low heat, stirring constantly. Set aside to cool.

3 Meanwhile, beat the eggs until light and fluffy. Gradually add the sugar and continue beating until blended. Sift over the flour, salt and baking powder, and fold to combine.

4 ▲ Stir in the cooled chocolate mixture. Add the vanilla and walnuts. Measure and set aside 475ml/16fl oz/ 2 cups of the chocolate mixture.

5 ▲ For the plain mixture, cream the butter and cream cheese with an electric mixer.

6 Add the sugar and continue beating until blended. Beat in the eggs, flour and vanilla.

7 Spread the unmeasured chocolate mixture in the tin. Pour over the plain mixture. Drop spoonfuls of the reserved chocolate mixture on top.

8 ▲ With a palette knife (metal spatula), swirl the mixtures to marble. Do not blend completely. Bake until just set, 35–40 minutes. Turn out when cool and cut into squares for serving.

Nutty Chocolate Squares

MAKES 16

2 eggs

10ml/2 tsp vanilla extract

pinch of salt

175g/6oz/1 cup pecan nuts,
  coarsely chopped

50g/2oz/1/2 cup plain (all-purpose) flour

50g/2oz/1/4 cup caster (superfine) sugar

120ml/4fl oz/1/2 cup golden
  (light corn) syrup

75g/3oz plain (semisweet) chocolate,
  finely chopped

45ml/3 tbsp butter

16 pecan halves, for decorating

1 Preheat the oven to 160°C/325°F/
Gas 3. Line the base and sides of a
20cm/8in square baking tin (pan) with
baking parchment and grease lightly.

2 ▼ Whisk together the eggs, vanilla
and salt. In another bowl, mix
together the pecan nuts and flour.
Set both aside.

3 In a pan, bring the sugar and
golden syrup to the boil. Remove
from the heat and stir in the
chocolate and butter and blend
thoroughly with a wooden spoon.

4 ▲ Mix in the beaten eggs, then
fold in the pecan mixture.

5 Pour the mixture into the prepared
tin and bake until set, about
35 minutes. Cool in the tin for
10 minutes before turning out. Cut
into 5cm/2in squares and press pecan
halves into the tops while warm. Cool
completely on a rack.

Raisin Brownies

MAKES 16

115g/4oz/1/2 cup butter or margarine

50g/2oz/1/2 cup unsweetened cocoa
  powder

2 eggs

225g/8oz/generous 1 cup caster
  (superfine) sugar

5ml/1 tsp vanilla extract

40g/11/2oz/1/3 cup plain (all-purpose) flour

75g/3oz/3/4 cup chopped walnuts

75g/3oz/2/3 cup raisins

1 Preheat the oven to 180°C/350°F/
Gas 4. Line the base and sides of a
20cm/8in square baking tin (pan)
with baking parchment and grease
the paper.

2 ▼ Gently melt the butter or
margarine in a small pan. Remove
from the heat and stir in the
cocoa powder.

3 With an electric mixer, beat the
eggs, sugar and vanilla together until
light. Add the cocoa mixture and stir
to blend.

4 ▲ Sift the flour over the cocoa
mixture and gently fold in. Add the
walnuts and raisins, and scrape the
mixture into the prepared tin.

5 Bake in the centre of the oven for
30 minutes. Do not overbake. Leave
in the tin to cool before cutting into
5cm/2in squares and removing. The
brownies should be soft and moist.

Nutty Chocolate Squares (top), Raisin Brownies

Chocolate Walnut Bars

MAKES 24

50g/2oz/¹/₃ cup walnuts

65g/2¹/₂oz/¹/₄ cup caster (superfine) sugar

115g/4oz/1 cup plain (all-purpose) flour, sifted

75g/3oz/6 tbsp cold unsalted (sweet) butter, cut into pieces

FOR THE TOPPING

25g/1oz/2 tbsp unsalted (sweet) butter

90ml/6 tbsp water

25g/1oz/¹/₄ cup unsweetened cocoa powder

90g/3¹/₂oz/¹/₂ cup caster sugar

5ml/1 tsp vanilla extract

pinch of salt

2 eggs

icing (confectioners') sugar, for dusting

1 Preheat the oven to 180°C/350°F/Gas 4. Grease the base and sides of a 20cm/8in square baking tin (pan).

2 ▼ Grind the walnuts with a few tablespoons of the sugar in a food processor, blender or coffee grinder.

3 In a bowl, combine the ground walnuts, remaining sugar and flour. With your fingertips, rub in the butter until the mixture resembles coarse breadcrumbs. Alternatively, process all the ingredients in a food processor until the mixture resembles coarse breadcrumbs.

4 ▲ Pat the walnut mixture into the base of the prepared tin in an even layer. Bake for 25 minutes.

5 ▲ Meanwhile, for the topping, melt the butter with the water. Whisk in the cocoa and sugar. Remove from the heat, stir in the vanilla and salt and let cool for 5 minutes. Whisk in the eggs until blended.

6 ▲ Pour the topping over the crust when baked.

7 Return to the oven and bake until set, about 20 minutes. Set the tin on a rack to cool. Cut into 6 × 2.5cm/2¹/₂ × 1in bars and dust with icing sugar. Store in the refrigerator.

Pecan Squares

MAKES 36

225g/8oz/2 cups plain (all-purpose) flour
pinch of salt
115g/4oz/generous ¹/₂ cup granulated sugar
225g/8oz/1 cup cold butter or margarine, chopped
1 egg
finely grated rind of 1 lemon
FOR THE TOPPING
175g/6oz/³/₄ cup butter
75g/3oz/scant ¹/₃ cup honey
50g/2oz/¹/₄ cup granulated sugar
115g/4oz/¹/₂ cup soft dark brown sugar
75ml/5 tbsp whipping cream
450g/1lb/2²/₃ cups pecan halves

1 Preheat the oven to 190°C/375°F/ Gas 5. Lightly grease a 38 × 27 × 2.5cm/ 15¹/₂ × 10¹/₂ × 1in Swiss roll tin (jelly roll pan).

2 ▲ Sift the flour and salt into a mixing bowl. Stir in the sugar. Cut and rub in the butter or margarine until the mixture resembles coarse breadcrumbs. Add the egg and lemon rind and blend with a fork until the mixture just holds together.

3 ▼ Spoon the mixture into the prepared tin. With floured fingertips, press into an even layer. Prick the pastry all over with a fork and chill for 10 minutes.

4 Bake the pastry crust for 15 minutes. Remove the tin from the oven, but keep the oven on while making the topping.

5 ▲ To make the topping, melt the butter, honey and both sugars. Bring to the boil. Boil, without stirring, for 2 minutes. Off the heat, stir in the cream and pecan halves. Pour over the crust, return to the oven and bake for 25 minutes. Leave to cool.

6 When cool, run a knife around the edge. Invert on to a baking sheet, place another sheet on top and invert again. Dip a sharp knife into very hot water and cut into squares for serving.

Figgy Bars

MAKES 48

350g/12oz/2 cups dried figs

3 eggs

175g/6oz/scant 1 cup caster (superfine) sugar

75g/3oz/²/₃ cup plain (all-purpose) flour

5ml/1 tsp baking powder

2.5ml/¹/₂ tsp ground cinnamon

1.5ml/¹/₄ tsp ground cloves

1.5ml/¹/₄ tsp freshly grated nutmeg

1.5ml/¹/₄ tsp salt

75g/3oz/³/₄ cup finely chopped walnuts

30ml/2 tbsp brandy or cognac

icing (confectioners') sugar, for dusting

1 Preheat the oven to 160°C/325°F/ Gas 3.

2 Line a 30 × 20 × 4cm/12 × 8 × 1¹/₂in tin (pan) with baking parchment and grease the paper.

3 ▲ With a sharp knife, chop the figs roughly. Set aside.

4 In a bowl, whisk the eggs and sugar until well blended. In another bowl, sift together the dry ingredients, then fold into the egg mixture in several batches.

5 ▼ Stir in the figs, walnuts and brandy or cognac.

6 Scrape the mixture into the prepared tin and bake until the top is firm and brown, 35–40 minutes. It should still be soft underneath.

7 Cool in the tin for 5 minutes, then turn out and transfer to a sheet of baking parchment lightly sprinkled with icing sugar. Cut into bars.

Lemon Bars

MAKES 36

50g/2oz/¹/₂ cup icing (confectioners') sugar

175g/6oz/1¹/₂ cups plain (all-purpose) flour

2.5ml/¹/₂ tsp salt

175g/6oz/³/₄ cup butter, cut in small pieces

FOR THE TOPPING

4 eggs

350g/12oz/1³/₄ cups caster (superfine) sugar

grated rind of 1 lemon

120ml/4fl oz/¹/₂ cup fresh lemon juice

175ml/6fl oz/³/₄ cup whipping cream

icing (confectioners') sugar, for dusting

1 Preheat the oven to 160°C/325°F/ Gas 3.

2 Grease a 33 × 23cm/13 × 9in baking tin (pan).

3 Sift the sugar, flour and salt into a bowl. With a pastry blender, cut in the butter until the mixture resembles coarse breadcrumbs.

4 ▲ Press the mixture into the base of the prepared tin (pan). Bake until golden brown, about 20 minutes.

5 Meanwhile, for the topping, whisk the eggs and sugar together until blended. Add the lemon rind and juice, and mix well.

6 ▲ Lightly whip the cream and fold into the egg mixture. Pour over the still-warm base, return to the oven, and bake until set, about 40 minutes.

7 Cool completely before cutting into bars. Dust with icing sugar.

Figgy Bars (top), Lemon Bars

Apricot Specials

MAKES 12

90g/3$\frac{1}{2}$oz/generous $\frac{1}{3}$ cup soft light
   brown sugar

75g/3oz/$\frac{2}{3}$ cup plain (all-purpose) flour

75g/3oz/6 tbsp cold unsalted (sweet)
   butter, cut in pieces

FOR THE TOPPING

150g/5oz/generous $\frac{1}{2}$ cup ready-to-eat
   dried apricots

250ml/8fl oz/1 cup water

grated rind of 1 lemon

55g/2$\frac{1}{2}$oz/5 tbsp caster (superfine) sugar

10ml/2 tsp cornflour (cornstarch)

50g/2oz/$\frac{1}{2}$ cup chopped walnuts

1 Preheat the oven to 180°C/350°F/
Gas 4.

2 ▲ In a bowl, combine the brown
sugar and flour. With a pastry blender,
cut in the butter until the mixture
resembles coarse breadcrumbs.

3 ▲ Transfer to a 20cm/8in square
baking tin (pan) and press level. Bake
for 15 minutes. Remove from the
oven but leave the oven on.

4 Meanwhile, for the topping,
combine the apricots and water in
a pan and simmer until soft, about
10 minutes. Strain the liquid and
reserve. Chop the apricots.

5 ▲ Return the apricots to the
pan and add the lemon rind, caster
sugar, cornflour, and 60ml/4 tbsp
of the soaking liquid. Cook for
1 minute.

6 ▲ Cool slightly before spreading
the topping over the base. Sprinkle
over the walnuts and continue baking
for 20 minutes more. Leave to cool in
the tin before cutting into bars.

Almond-topped Squares

MAKES 18

75g/3oz/²/₃ cup butter

50g/2oz/¹/₄ cup granulated sugar

1 egg yolk

grated rind and juice of ¹/₂ lemon

2.5ml/¹/₂ tsp vanilla extract

30ml/2 tbsp whipping cream

115g/4oz/1 cup plain (all-purpose) flour

FOR THE TOPPING

225g/8oz/generous 1 cup granulated sugar

75g/3oz/³/₄ cup flaked (sliced) almonds

4 egg whites

2.5ml/¹/₂ tsp ground ginger

2.5ml/¹/₂ tsp ground cinnamon

1 ▲ Preheat the oven to 190°C/375°F/ Gas 5. Line a 33 × 23cm/13 × 9in Swiss roll tin (jelly roll pan) with baking parchment; grease the paper.

2 Cream the butter and sugar. Beat in the egg yolk, lemon rind and juice, vanilla extract and cream.

3 ▲ Gradually stir in the flour. Gather into a ball of dough.

4 With lightly floured fingers, press the dough into the prepared tin. Bake for 15 minutes. Remove from the oven but leave the oven on.

5 ▲ To make the topping, combine all the ingredients in a heavy pan. Cook, stirring until the mixture comes to the boil.

6 Continue boiling until just golden, about 1 minute. Pour over the dough, spreading evenly.

7 ▲ Return to the oven and bake for about 45 minutes. Remove and score into bars or squares. Cool completely before cutting into squares and serving.

Spiced Raisin Bars

MAKES 30

115g/4oz/1 cup plain (all-purpose) flour

7.5ml/1½ tsp baking powder

5ml/1 tsp ground cinnamon

2.5ml/½ tsp freshly grated nutmeg

1.5ml/¼ tsp ground cloves

1.5ml/¼ tsp ground allspsice

200g/7oz/1½ cups raisins

115g/4oz/½ cup butter or margarine,
    at room temperature

90g/3½oz/½ cup sugar

2 eggs

165g/5½oz/scant ½ cup black treacle
    (molasses)

50g/2oz/⅓ cup walnuts, chopped

1 Preheat the oven to 180°C/350°F/
Gas 4. Line a 33 × 23cm/13 × 9in tin
(pan) with baking parchment; grease.

2 Sift together the flour, baking
powder and spices.

3 ▲ Place the raisins in another bowl
and toss with a few tablespoons of the
flour mixture.

4 ▲ With an electric mixer, cream
the butter or margarine and sugar
together until light and fluffy. Beat
in the eggs, one at a time, then the
molasses. Stir in the flour mixture,
raisins and walnuts.

5 Spread evenly in the tin. Bake until
just set, 15–18 minutes. Cool in the
tin before cutting into bars.

Toffee Meringue Bars

MAKES 12

50g/2oz/¼ cup butter

215g/7½oz/scant 1 cup soft dark
    brown sugar

1 egg

2.5ml/½ tsp vanilla extract

65g/2½oz/9 tbsp plain (all-purpose) flour

2.5ml/½ tsp salt

1.5ml/¼ tsp freshly grated nutmeg

FOR THE TOPPING

1 egg white

pinch of salt

15ml/l tbsp golden (light corn) syrup

90g/3½oz/½ cup caster (superfine) sugar

50g/2oz/⅓ cup walnuts, finely chopped

1 ▲ Combine the butter and brown
sugar in a pan and heat until
bubbling. Set aside to cool.

2 Preheat the oven to 180°C/350°F/
Gas 4. Line the base and sides of a
20cm/8in square cake tin (pan) with
baking parchment and grease.

3 Beat the egg and vanilla into the
cooled sugar mixture. Sift over the
flour, salt and nutmeg, and fold in.
Spread in the base of the tin.

4 ▲ For the topping, beat the egg white
with the salt until it holds soft peaks.
Beat in the golden syrup, then the
sugar and continue beating until
the mixture holds stiff peaks. Fold
in the nuts and spread on top. Bake
for 30 minutes. Cut into bars when cool.

Spiced Raisin Bars (top), Toffee Meringue Bars

BUNS & TEA BREADS

EASY TO MAKE AND SATISFYING TO
EAT, THESE BUNS AND TEA BREADS
WILL FILL THE HOUSE WITH
MOUTHWATERING SCENTS AND LURE
YOUR FAMILY AND FRIENDS TO
LINGER OVER BREAKFAST, COFFEE
OR TEA – AND THEY ARE GREAT FOR
SNACKS OR LUNCH.

Blueberry Muffins

Makes 12

185g/6¹/₂oz/1²/₃ cups plain
(all-purpose) flour

65g/2¹/₂oz/5 tbsp caster (superfine) sugar

10ml/2 tsp baking powder

1.5ml/¹/₄ tsp salt

2 eggs

50g/2oz/¹/₄ cup butter, melted

175ml/6fl oz/³/₄ cup milk

5ml/1 tsp vanilla extract

5ml/1 tsp grated lemon rind

175g/6oz/1¹/₂ cups fresh blueberries

1 Preheat the oven to 200°C/400°F/ Gas 6.

2 ▼ Grease a 12-cup muffin tray.

3 ▲ Sift the flour, sugar, baking powder and salt into a bowl.

4 In another bowl, whisk the eggs until blended. Add the melted butter, milk, vanilla and lemon rind, and stir to combine.

5 Make a well in the dry ingredients and pour in the egg mixture. With a large metal spoon, stir just until the flour is moistened, not until smooth.

6 ▲ Fold in the blueberries.

7 ▲ Spoon the batter into the tray, leaving room for the muffins to rise.

8 Bake until the tops spring back when touched lightly, 20–25 minutes. Leave to cool in the tray for 5 minutes before turning out.

Apple and Cranberry Muffins

MAKES 12

50g/2oz/¹/₄ cup butter or margarine
1 egg
90g/3¹/₂oz/¹/₂ cup caster (superfine) sugar
grated rind of 1 large orange
120ml/4fl oz/¹/₂ cup freshly squeezed orange juice
150g/5oz/1¹/₄ cups plain (all-purpose) flour
5ml/1 tsp baking powder
2.5ml/¹/₂ tsp bicarbonate of soda (baking soda)
5ml/1 tsp ground cinnamon
2.5ml/¹/₂ tsp freshly grated nutmeg
2.5ml/¹/₂ tsp ground allspice
1.5ml/¹/₄ tsp ground ginger
1.5ml/¹/₄ tsp salt
1–2 eating apples
150g/6oz/1¹/₂ cups cranberries
50g/2oz/¹/₃ cup walnuts, chopped
icing (confectioners') sugar, for dusting (optional)

1 Preheat the oven to 180°C/350°F/ Gas 4. Grease a 12-cup muffin tray or use paper cases.

2 Melt the butter or margarine over gentle heat. Set aside to cool.

3 ▲ Place the egg in a mixing bowl and whisk lightly. Add the melted butter or margarine and whisk to combine.

4 Add the sugar, orange rind and juice. Whisk to blend, then set aside.

5 In a large bowl, sift together the flour, baking powder, bicarbonate of soda, cinnamon, nutmeg, allspice, ginger and salt. Set aside.

6 ▲ Quarter, core and peel the apples. With a sharp knife, chop coarsely.

7 Make a well in the dry ingredients and pour in the egg mixture. With a spoon, stir until just blended.

8 ▲ Add the apples, cranberries and walnuts, and stir to blend.

9 Fill the cups three-quarters full and bake until the tops spring back when touched lightly, 25–30 minutes. Transfer to a rack to cool. Dust with icing sugar, if you like.

Chocolate Chip Muffins

MAKES 10

115g/4oz/1/2 cup butter or margarine, at room temperature

65g/2 1/2oz/5 tbsp caster (superfine) sugar

25g/1oz/2 tbsp soft dark brown sugar

2 eggs, at room temperature

215g/7 1/2oz/scant 2 cups plain (all-purpose) flour

5ml/1 tsp baking powder

120ml/4fl oz/1/2 cup milk

175g/6oz/ plain chocolate chips

1 Preheat the oven to 190°C/375°F/ Gas 5. Grease 10 muffin cups or use paper cases.

2 ▼ With an electric mixer, cream the butter or margarine until soft. Add both sugars and beat until light and fluffy. Beat in the eggs, one at a time.

3 Sift together the flour and baking powder, twice. Fold into the butter mixture, alternating with the milk.

4 ▲ Divide half the mixture between the muffin cups. Sprinkle several chocolate chips on top, then cover with a spoonful of the batter. To ensure even baking, half-fill any empty cups with water.

5 Bake until lightly coloured, about 25 minutes. Leave to stand for 5 minutes before turning out.

Chocolate Walnut Muffins

MAKES 12

175g/6oz/3/4 cup unsalted (sweet) butter

150g/5oz plain (semisweet) chocolate

200g/7oz/1 cup caster (superfine) sugar

50g/2oz/1/4 cup soft dark brown sugar

4 eggs

5ml/1 tsp vanilla extract

1.5ml/1/4 tsp almond extract

90g/3 1/2oz/3/4 cup plain (all-purpose) flour

15ml/1 tbsp unsweetened cocoa powder

115g/4oz/2/3 cup walnuts, chopped

1 Preheat the oven to 180°C/350°F/ Gas 4. Grease a 12-cup muffin tray or use paper cases.

2 ▼ Melt the butter with the chocolate in the top of a double boiler or in a heatproof bowl set over a pan of hot water. Transfer to a large mixing bowl.

3 Stir both the sugars into the chocolate mixture. Mix in the eggs, one at a time, then add the vanilla and almond extracts.

4 Sift over the flour and cocoa.

5 ▲ Fold in and stir in the walnuts.

6 Fill the prepared cups almost to the top and bake until a skewer inserted in the centre barely comes out clean, 30–35 minutes. Leave to stand for 5 minutes before turning out on to a rack to cool completely.

Chocolate Chip Muffins (top), Chocolate Walnut Muffins

Raisin Bran Buns

MAKES 15

50g/2oz/¹/₄ cup butter or margarine

40g/1¹/₂oz/¹/₃ cup plain (all-purpose) flour

50g/2oz/¹/₂ cup wholemeal (whole-wheat) flour

7.5ml/1¹/₂ tsp bicarbonate of soda (baking soda)

pinch of salt

5ml/1 tsp ground cinnamon

25g/1oz/¹/₄ cup bran

75g/3oz/generous ¹/₂ cup raisins

65g/2¹/₂oz/5 tbsp soft dark brown sugar

50g/2oz/¹/₄ cup caster (superfine) sugar

1 egg

250ml/8fl oz/1 cup buttermilk

juice of ¹/₂ lemon

1 Preheat the oven to 200°C/400°F/ Gas 6. Grease 15 bun-tray cups.

2 ▲ Place the butter or margarine in a pan and melt over gentle heat. Set aside.

3 In a mixing bowl, sift together the flours, bicarbonate of soda, salt and cinnamon.

4 ▲ Add the bran, raisins and sugars and stir until blended.

5 In another bowl, mix together the egg, buttermilk, lemon juice and melted butter.

6 ▲ Add the buttermilk mixture to the dry ingredients and stir lightly and quickly until just moistened; do not mix until smooth.

7 ▲ Spoon the mixture into the prepared bun tray, filling the cups almost to the top. Half-fill any empty cups with water.

8 Bake until golden, 15–20 minutes. Serve warm or at room temperature.

Raspberry Crumble Buns

MAKES 12

175g/6oz/1$^{1}/_{2}$ cups plain (all-purpose) flour
50g/2oz/$^{1}/_{4}$ cup caster (superfine) sugar
50g/2oz/$^{1}/_{4}$ cup soft light brown sugar
10ml/2 tsp baking powder
pinch of salt
5ml/1 tsp ground cinnamon
115g/4oz/$^{1}/_{2}$ cup butter, melted
1 egg
120ml/4fl oz/$^{1}/_{2}$ cup milk
150g/5oz/scant 1 cup fresh raspberries
grated rind of 1 lemon
FOR THE CRUMBLE TOPPING
25g/1oz/$^{1}/_{4}$ cup finely chopped pecan nuts or walnuts
50g/2oz/$^{1}/_{4}$ cup soft dark brown sugar
20g/$^{3}/_{4}$oz/3 tbsp plain (all-purpose) flour
5ml/1 tsp ground cinnamon
40g/1$^{1}/_{2}$oz/3 tbsp butter, melted

1 Preheat the oven to 180°C/350°F/ Gas 4. Lightly grease a 12-cup bun tray or use paper cases.

2 Sift the flour into a bowl. Add the sugars, baking powder, salt and cinnamon, and stir to blend.

3 ▲ Make a well in the centre. Place the butter, egg and milk in the well and mix until just combined. Stir in the raspberries and lemon rind. Spoon the mixture into the prepared bun tray, filling the cups almost to the top.

4 ▼ For the crumble topping, mix the nuts, dark brown sugar, flour and cinnamon in a bowl. Add the melted butter and stir to blend.

5 ▲ Spoon some of the crumble over each bun. Bake until browned, about 25 minutes. Transfer to a rack to cool slightly. Serve warm.

Carrot Buns

Makes 12

175g/6oz/3/4 cup margarine,
  at room temperature

90g/3½oz/generous ⅓ cup soft dark
  brown sugar

1 egg, at room temperature

15ml/1 tbsp water

225g/8oz/1 cup carrots, grated

150g/5oz/1¼ cups plain (all-purpose) flour

5ml/1 tsp baking powder

2.5ml/½ tsp bicarbonate of soda
  (baking soda)

5ml/1 tsp ground cinnamon

1.5ml/¼ tsp freshly grated nutmeg

2.5ml/½ tsp salt

1 Preheat the oven to 180°C/350°F/
Gas 4. Grease a 12-cup bun tray or
use paper cases.

2 With an electric mixer, cream the
margarine and sugar until light and
fluffy. Beat in the egg and water.

3 ▲ Stir in the carrots.

4 Sift over the flour, baking powder,
bicarbonate of soda, cinnamon,
nutmeg and salt. Stir to blend.

5 ▼ Spoon the mixture into the
prepared bun tray, filling the cups
almost to the top. Bake until the tops
spring back when touched lightly,
about 35 minutes. Leave to stand for
10 minutes before transferring to a rack.

Dried Cherry Buns

Makes 16

250ml/8fl oz/1 cup natural (plain) yogurt

175g/6oz/3/4 cup dried cherries

115g/4oz/½ cup butter, at
  room temperature

175g/6oz/scant 1 cup caster
  (superfine) sugar

2 eggs, at room temperature

5ml/1 tsp vanilla essence (extract)

200g/7oz/1¾ cups plain (all-purpose) flour

10ml/2 tsp baking powder

5ml/1 tsp bicarbonate of soda (baking soda)

pinch of salt

1 In a mixing bowl, combine the
yogurt and cherries. Cover and leave
to stand for 30 minutes.

2 Preheat the oven to 180°C/350°F/
Gas 4. Grease 16 bun-tray cups or use
paper cases.

3 With an electric mixer, cream the
butter and sugar together until light
and fluffy.

4 ▼ Add the eggs, one at a time,
beating well after each addition. Add
the vanilla and the cherry mixture and
stir to blend. Set aside.

5 ▲ In another bowl, sift together
the flour, baking powder, bicarbonate
of soda and salt. Fold into the cherry
mixture in three batches.

6 Fill the prepared cups two-thirds
full. For even baking, half-fill any
empty cups with water. Bake until
the tops spring back when touched
lightly, about 20 minutes. Transfer
to a rack to cool.

Carrot Buns (top), Dried Cherry Buns

Oat and Raisin Muffins

MAKES 12

75g/3oz/scant 1 cup rolled oats

250ml/8fl oz/1 cup buttermilk

115g/4oz/¹/₂ cup butter, at
    room temperature

90g/3¹/₂oz/generous ¹/₃ cup soft dark
    brown sugar

1 egg, at room temperature

115g/4oz/1 cup plain (all-purpose) flour

5ml/1 tsp baking powder

2.5ml/¹/₂ tsp bicarbonate of soda
    (baking soda)

1.5ml/¹/₄ tsp salt

25g/1oz/2 tbsp raisins

~ COOK'S TIP ~

If buttermilk is not available, add
5ml/1 tsp lemon juice or vinegar
to milk. Let the mixture stand
for a few minutes to curdle.

1 ▲ In a bowl, combine the oats and buttermilk, and leave to soak for 1 hour.

2 ▲ Lightly grease a 12-cup muffin tray or use paper cases.

3 ▲ Preheat the oven to 200°C/400°F/Gas 6. With an electric mixer, cream the butter and sugar until light and fluffy. Beat in the egg.

4 In another bowl, sift the flour, baking powder, bicarbonate of soda and salt. Stir into the butter mixture, alternating with the oat mixture. Fold in the raisins. Do not overmix.

5 Fill the prepared cups two-thirds full. Bake until a skewer inserted in the centre comes out clean, 20–25 minutes. Transfer to a rack to cool.

Pumpkin Muffins

MAKES 14

115g/4oz/¹/₂ cup butter or margarine,
    at room temperature

150g/5oz/²/₃ cup soft dark brown sugar

60ml/4 tbsp black treacle (molasses)

1 egg, at room temperature, beaten

225g/8oz cooked or canned pumpkin

225g/8oz/2 cups plain (all-purpose) flour

1.5ml/¹/₄ tsp salt

5ml/1 tsp bicarbonate of soda
    (baking soda)

7.5ml/1¹/₂ tsp ground cinnamon

5ml/1 tsp freshly grated nutmeg

25g/1oz/2 tbsp currants or raisins

1 Preheat the oven to 200°C/400°F/Gas 6. Grease 14 muffin cups or use paper cases.

2 With an electric mixer, cream the butter or margarine until soft. Add the sugar and molasses and beat until light and fluffy.

3 ▲ Add the egg and pumpkin and stir until well blended.

4 Sift over the flour, salt, bicarbonate of soda, cinnamon and nutmeg. Fold just enough to blend; do not overmix.

5 ▼ Fold in the currants or raisins.

6 Spoon the mixture into the prepared muffin cups, filling them three-quarters full.

7 Bake until the tops spring back when touched lightly, 12–15 minutes. Serve warm or cold.

Prune Muffins

MAKES 12

1 egg
250ml/8fl oz/1 cup milk
120ml/4fl oz/½ cup vegetable oil
50g/2oz/¼ cup caster (superfine) sugar
25g/1oz/2 tbsp soft dark brown sugar
275g/10oz/2½ cups plain (all-purpose) flour
10ml/2 tsp baking powder
2.5ml/½ tsp salt
1.5ml/¼ tsp grated nutmeg
115g/4oz/½ cup cooked pitted prunes, chopped

1 Preheat the oven to 200°C/400°F/Gas 6. Grease a 12-cup muffin tray.

2 Break the egg into a mixing bowl and beat with a fork. Beat in the milk and oil.

3 ▼ Stir in the sugars. Set aside.

4 Sift the flour, baking powder, salt and nutmeg into a mixing bowl. Make a well in the centre, pour in the egg mixture and stir until moistened. Do not overmix; the batter should be slightly lumpy.

5 ▲ Fold in the prunes.

6 Fill the prepared cups two-thirds full. Bake until golden brown, about 20 minutes. Leave to stand for 10 minutes before turning out. Serve warm or at room temperature.

Yogurt and Honey Muffins

MAKES 12

50g/2oz/¼ cup butter
75ml/5 tbsp clear honey
250ml/8fl oz/1 cup natural (plain) yogurt
1 large egg, at room temperature
grated rind of 1 lemon
50ml/2fl oz/¼ cup lemon juice
150g/5oz/1¼ cups plain (all-purpose) flour
175g/6oz/1⅔ cups wholemeal (whole-wheat) flour
7.5ml/1½ tsp bicarbonate of soda (baking soda)
pinch of freshly grated nutmeg

~ **VARIATION** ~

For Walnut Yogurt Honey Muffins, add 50g/2oz/½ cup chopped walnuts, folded in with the flour. This makes a more substantial muffin.

1 Preheat the oven to 190°C/375°F/Gas 5. Grease a 12-cup muffin tray or use paper cases.

2 In a pan, melt the butter and honey. Remove from the heat and set aside to cool slightly.

3 ▲ In a bowl, whisk together the yogurt, egg, lemon rind and juice. Add the butter and honey mixture. Set aside.

4 ▲ In another bowl, sift together the dry ingredients.

5 Fold the dry ingredients into the yogurt mixture to blend.

6 Fill the prepared cups two-thirds full. Bake until the tops spring back when touched lightly, 20–25 minutes. Cool in the tray for 5 minutes before turning out. Serve warm or at room temperature.

Prune Muffins (top), Yogurt and Honey Muffins

Banana Muffins

MAKES 10

250g/9oz/2$\frac{1}{4}$ cups plain (all-purpose) flour

5ml/1 tsp baking powder

5ml/1 tsp bicarbonate of soda
(baking soda)

1.5ml/$\frac{1}{4}$ tsp salt

2.5ml/$\frac{1}{2}$ tsp ground cinnamon

1.5ml/$\frac{1}{4}$ tsp freshly grated nutmeg

3 large ripe bananas

1 egg

65g/2$\frac{1}{2}$oz/scant $\frac{1}{3}$ cup soft dark
brown sugar

50ml/2fl oz/$\frac{1}{4}$ cup vegetable oil

25g/1oz/2 tbsp raisins

1 ▼ Preheat the oven to 190°C/ 375°F/Gas 5. Lightly grease or line ten deep muffin cups with paper cases.

2 Sift together the flour, baking powder, bicarbonate of soda, salt, cinnamon and nutmeg. Set aside.

3 ▲ With an electric mixer, beat the peeled bananas at moderate speed until mashed.

4 ▲ Beat in the egg, sugar and oil.

5 Add the dry ingredients and beat in gradually, on low speed. Mix just until blended. With a wooden spoon, stir in the raisins.

6 Fill the prepared cups two-thirds full. For even baking, half-fill any empty cups with water.

7 ▲ Bake until the tops spring back when touched lightly, 20–25 minutes. Transfer to a rack to cool.

Maple Pecan Muffins

MAKES 20

175g/6oz/1 cup pecan nuts
350g/12oz/3 cups plain (all-purpose) flour
5ml/1 tsp baking powder
5ml/1 tsp bicarbonate of soda (baking soda)
1.5ml/^{1}/$_4$ tsp salt
1.5ml/^{1}/$_4$ tsp ground cinnamon
90g/3^1/$_2$oz/^{1}/$_2$ cup caster (superfine) sugar
65g/2^1/$_2$oz/scant ^{1}/$_3$ cup soft light brown sugar
45ml/3 tbsp maple syrup
150g/5oz/10 tbsp butter, at room temperature
3 eggs, at room temperature
300ml/^{1}/$_2$ pint/1^1/$_4$ cups buttermilk
60 pecan halves, for decorating

1 Preheat the oven to 180°C/350°F/ Gas 4. Lightly grease 20 deep muffin cups or use paper cases.

2 ▲ Spread the pecan nuts on a baking sheet and toast in the oven for 5 minutes. When cool, chop coarsely and set aside.

~ VARIATION ~

For Pecan Spice Muffins, substitute an equal quantity of golden (light corn) syrup for the maple syrup. Increase the cinnamon to 2.5ml/^{1}/$_2$ tsp, and add 5ml/1 tsp ground ginger and 2.5ml/^{1}/$_2$ tsp freshly grated nutmeg, sifted with the dry ingredients.

3 In a bowl, sift together the flour, baking powder, bicarbonate of soda, salt and cinnamon. Set aside.

4 ▲ In a large mixing bowl, combine the caster sugar, light brown sugar, maple syrup and butter. Beat with an electric mixer until light and fluffy.

5 Add the eggs, one at a time, beating to incorporate thoroughly after each addition.

6 ▲ Pour half the buttermilk and half the dry ingredients into the butter mixture, then stir until blended. Repeat with the remaining buttermilk and dry ingredients.

7 Fold in the chopped pecan nuts. Fill the prepared cups two-thirds full. Top with the pecan halves. For even baking, half-fill any empty cups with water.

8 Bake until puffed up and golden, 20–25 minutes. Leave to stand for 5 minutes before turning out.

Cheese Muffins

MAKES 9

50g/2oz/¹/₄ cup butter
200g/7oz/1³/₄ cups plain (all-purpose) flour
10ml/2 tsp baking powder
30ml/2 tbsp sugar
1.5ml/¹/₄ tsp salt
5ml/1 tsp paprika
2 eggs
120ml/4fl oz/¹/₂ cup milk
5ml/1 tsp dried thyme
50g/2oz/¹/₂ cup mature Cheddar cheese, cut into 1cm/¹/₂in dice

1 Preheat the oven to 190°C/375°F/ Gas 5. Thickly grease nine deep muffin cups or use paper cases.

2 Melt the butter and set aside.

3 ▼ In a mixing bowl, sift together the flour, baking powder, sugar, salt and paprika.

4 ▲ In another bowl, combine the eggs, milk, melted butter and thyme, and whisk to blend.

5 Add the milk mixture to the dry ingredients and stir until just moistened; do not mix until smooth.

6 ▲ Place a heaped spoonful of batter into the prepared cups. Drop a few pieces of cheese over each, then top with another spoonful of batter. For even baking, half-fill any empty muffin cups with water.

7 ▲ Bake until puffed and golden, about 25 minutes. Leave to stand for 5 minutes before turning out on to a rack. Serve warm or at room temperature.

Bacon and Cornmeal Muffins

MAKES 14

8 bacon rashers (strips)
50g/2oz/¹/₄ cup butter
50g/2oz/¹/₄ cup margarine
115g/4oz/1 cup plain (all-purpose) flour
15ml/1 tbsp baking powder
5ml/1 tsp sugar
1.5ml/¹/₄ tsp salt
225g/8oz/2 cups cornmeal
120ml/4fl oz/¹/₂ cup milk
2 eggs

1 Preheat the oven to 200°C/400°F/ Gas 6. Lightly grease 14 deep muffin cups or use paper cases.

2 ▲ Fry the bacon until crisp. Drain on kitchen paper, then chop into small pieces. Set aside.

3 Gently melt the butter and margarine, and set aside.

4 ▲ Sift the flour, baking powder, sugar, and salt into a large mixing bowl. Stir in the cornmeal, then make a well in the centre.

5 In a pan, heat the milk to lukewarm. In a small bowl, lightly whisk the eggs, then add to the milk. Stir in the melted fats.

6 ▼ Pour the milk mixture into the centre of the well and stir until smooth and well blended.

7 ▲ Stir the bacon into the mixture, then spoon the mixture into the prepared cups, filling them half-full. Bake until risen and lightly coloured, about 20 minutes. Serve hot or warm.

Corn Bread

MAKES 1 LOAF

115g/4oz/1 cup plain (all-purpose) flour
65g/2¹/₂oz/5 tbsp caster (superfine) sugar
5ml/1 tsp salt
15ml/1 tbsp baking powder
175g/6oz/1¹/₂ cups cornmeal or polenta
350ml/12fl oz/1¹/₂ cups milk
2 eggs
75g/3oz/6 tbsp butter, melted
115g/4oz/¹/₂ cup margarine, melted

1 Preheat the oven to 200°C/400°F/ Gas 6. Line a 23 × 13cm/9 × 5in loaf tin (pan) with baking parchment and grease.

2 Sift the flour, sugar, salt and baking powder into a mixing bowl.

3 ▼ Add the cornmeal and stir to blend. Make a well in the centre.

4 ▲ Whisk together the milk, eggs, butter and margarine. Pour the mixture into the well. Stir until just blended; do not overmix.

5 Pour into the tin and bake until a skewer inserted into the centre comes out clean, about 45 minutes. Serve hot or at room temperature.

Spicy Corn Bread

MAKES 9 SQUARES

3–4 whole canned chilli peppers, drained
2 eggs
450ml/³/₄ pint/scant 2 cups buttermilk
50g/2oz/¹/₄ cup butter, melted
50g/2oz/¹/₂ cup plain (all-purpose) flour
5ml/1 tsp bicarbonate of soda (baking soda)
10ml/2 tsp salt
175g/6oz/1¹/₂ cups cornmeal, or polenta
350g/12oz/2 cups canned corn, drained, or frozen corn, thawed

1 Preheat the oven to 200°C/400°F/ Gas 6. Line the bottom and sides of a 23cm/9in square cake tin (pan) with baking parchment and grease lightly.

2 ▲ With a sharp knife, finely chop the chillies and set aside.

3 ▲ In a large bowl, whisk the eggs until frothy, then whisk in the buttermilk. Add the melted butter.

4 In another large bowl, sift together the flour, bicarbonate of soda and salt. Fold into the buttermilk mixture in three batches, then fold in the cornmeal in three batches.

5 ▲ Fold in the chillies and corn.

6 Pour the mixture into the prepared tin and bake until a skewer inserted in the middle comes out clean, 25–30 minutes. Leave to stand for 2–3 minutes before turning out. Cut into squares and serve warm.

Corn Bread (top), Spicy Corn Bread

Fruity Tea Bread

Makes 1 loaf

225g/8oz/2 cups plain (all-purpose) flour

115g/4oz/generous 1/2 cup caster (superfine) sugar

15ml/1 tbsp baking powder

2.5ml/1/2 tsp salt

grated rind of 1 large orange

170ml/51/2fl oz/scant 3/4 cup fresh orange juice

2 eggs, lightly beaten

75g/3oz/6 tbsp butter or margarine, melted

115g/4oz/1 cup fresh cranberries, or bilberries

50g/2oz/1/2 cup chopped walnuts

1 Preheat the oven to 180°C/350°F/ Gas 4. Line a 23 × 13cm/9 × 5in loaf tin (pan) with baking parchment and grease.

2 Sift the flour, sugar, baking powder and salt into a mixing bowl.

3 ▼ Stir in the orange rind.

4 ▲ Make a well in the centre and add the orange juice, eggs and melted butter or margarine. Stir from the centre until the ingredients are blended; do not overmix.

5 ▲ Add the berries and walnuts, and stir until blended.

6 Transfer the mixture to the prepared tin and bake until a skewer inserted into the centre comes out clean, 45–50 minutes.

7 ▲ Leave to cool in the tin for 10 minutes before transferring to a rack to cool completely. Serve thinly sliced, toasted or plain, with butter or cream cheese and jam.

Date and Pecan Loaf

MAKES 1 LOAF

175g/6oz/1 cup pitted dates, chopped
175ml/6fl oz/³/4 cup boiling water
50g/2oz/¹/4 cup unsalted (sweet) butter, at room temperature
50g/2oz/¹/4 cup soft dark brown sugar
50g/2oz/¹/4 cup caster (superfine) sugar
1 egg, at room temperature
30ml/2 tbsp brandy
165g/5¹/2oz/1¹/4 cups plain (all-purpose) flour
10ml/2 tsp baking powder
2.5ml/¹/2 tsp salt
4ml/³/4 tsp freshly grated nutmeg
75g/3oz/³/4 cup coarsely chopped pecan nuts or walnuts

1 ▲ Place the dates in a bowl and pour over the boiling water. Set aside to cool.

2 Preheat the oven to 180°C/350°F/ Gas 4. Line a 23 × 13cm/9 × 5in loaf tin (pan) with baking parchment and grease.

3 ▲ With an electric mixer, cream the butter and sugars until light and fluffy. Beat in the egg and brandy, then set aside.

4 Sift the flour, baking powder, salt and nutmeg together, three times.

5 ▼ Fold the dry ingredients into the sugar mixture in three batches, alternating with the dates and water.

6 ▲ Fold in the nuts.

7 Pour the mixture into the prepared tin and bake until a skewer inserted into the centre comes out clean, 45–50 minutes. Leave to cool in the tin for 10 minutes before transferring to a rack to cool completely.

Orange and Honey Tea Bread

MAKES 1 LOAF

375g/13oz/3¼ cups plain (all-purpose) flour

12.5ml/2½ tsp baking powder

2.5ml/½ tsp bicarbonate of soda (baking soda)

2.5ml/½ tsp salt

25g/1oz/2 tbsp margarine

250ml/8fl oz/1 cup clear honey

1 egg, at room temperature, lightly beaten

25ml/1½ tbsp grated orange rind

175ml/6fl oz/¾ cup freshly squeezed orange juice

115g/4oz/1 cup walnuts, chopped

1 Preheat the oven to 160°C/325°F/ Gas 3.

2 Sift together the flour, baking powder, bicarbonate of soda and salt.

3 Line the bottom and sides of a 23 × 13cm/9 × 5in loaf tin (pan) with baking parchment and grease.

4 ▲ With an electric mixer, cream the margarine until soft. Stir in the honey until blended, then stir in the egg. Add the orange rind and stir to combine thoroughly.

5 ▲ Fold the flour mixture into the honey and egg mixture in three batches, alternating with the orange juice. Stir in the walnuts.

6 Pour into the tin and bake until a skewer inserted into the centre comes out clean, 60–70 minutes. Leave to stand for 10 minutes before turning out on to a rack to cool.

Apple Loaf

MAKES 1 LOAF

1 egg

250ml/8fl oz/1 cup bottled or homemade apple sauce

50g/2oz/¼ cup butter or margarine, melted

115g/4oz/½ cup soft dark brown sugar

50g/2oz/¼ cup caster (superfine) sugar

275g/10oz/2½ cups plain (all-purpose) flour

10ml/2 tsp baking powder

2.5ml/½ tsp bicarbonate of soda (baking soda)

2.5ml/½ tsp salt

5ml/1 tsp ground cinnamon

2.5ml/½ tsp freshly grated nutmeg

65g/2½oz/½ cup currants or raisins

50g/2oz/⅓ cup pecan nuts or walnuts, chopped

1 Preheat the oven to 180°C/350°F/ Gas 4. Line a 23 × 13cm/9 × 5in loaf tin (pan) with baking parchment and grease.

2 ▲ Break the egg into a bowl and beat lightly. Stir in the apple sauce, butter or margarine and both sugars. Set aside.

3 In another bowl, sift together the flour, baking powder, bicarbonate of soda, salt, cinnamon and nutmeg. Fold the dry ingredients into the apple sauce mixture in three batches.

4 ▼ Stir in the currants or raisins, and nuts.

5 Pour into the prepared tin and bake until a skewer inserted into the centre comes out clean, about 1 hour. Leave to stand for 10 minutes. Turn out on to a rack and cool completely.

Orange and Honey Tea Bread (top), Apple Loaf

Lemon and Walnut Tea Bread

MAKES 1 LOAF

115g/4oz/^{1}/$_2$ cup butter or margarine, at room temperature
90g/3^1/$_2$oz/^{1}/$_2$ cup sugar
2 eggs, at room temperature, separated
grated rind of 2 lemons
30ml/2 tbsp lemon juice
225g/8oz/2 cups plain (all-purpose) flour
10ml/2 tsp baking powder
120ml/4fl oz/^{1}/$_2$ cup milk
50g/2oz/^{1}/$_3$ cup walnuts, chopped
pinch of salt

1 Preheat the oven to 180°C/350°F/ Gas 4. Line a 23 × 13cm/9 × 5in loaf tin (pan) with baking parchment and grease.

2 With an electric mixer, cream the butter or margarine with the sugar until light and fluffy.

3 ▲ Beat in the egg yolks.

4 Add the lemon rind and juice, and stir until blended. Set aside.

5 ▲ In another bowl, sift together the flour and baking powder, three times. Fold into the butter mixture in three batches, alternating with the milk. Fold in the walnuts. Set aside.

6 ▲ Beat the egg whites and salt until stiff peaks form. Fold a large dollop of the egg whites into the walnut mixture to lighten it. Fold in the remaining egg whites carefully until just blended.

7 ▲ Pour the batter into the prepared tin and bake until a skewer inserted into the centre of the loaf comes out clean, 45–50 minutes. Leave to stand for 5 minutes before turning out on to a rack to cool completely.

Wholemeal Banana Nut Loaf

MAKES 1 LOAF

115g/4oz/¹/₂ cup butter, at room temperature

115g/4oz/generous ¹/₂ cup caster (superfine) sugar

2 eggs, at room temperature

115g/4oz/1 cup plain (all-purpose) flour

5ml/1 tsp bicarbonate of soda (baking soda)

1.5ml/¹/₄ tsp salt

5ml/1 tsp ground cinnamon

50g/2oz/¹/₂ cup wholemeal (whole-wheat) flour

3 large ripe bananas

5ml/1 tsp vanilla extract

50g/2oz/¹/₃ cup chopped walnuts

1 Preheat the oven to 180°C/350°F/ Gas 4. Line the base and sides of a 23 × 13cm/9 × 5in loaf tin (pan) with baking parchment and grease the paper.

2 With an electric mixer, cream the butter and sugar together until light and fluffy.

3 ▲ Add the eggs, one at a time, beating well after each addition.

4 Sift the plain flour, bicarbonate of soda, salt and cinnamon over the butter mixture and stir to blend.

5 ▲ Stir in the wholemeal flour.

6 ▲ With a fork, mash the bananas to a purée, then stir into the mixture. Stir in the vanilla and nuts.

7 ▲ Pour the mixture into the prepared tin and spread level.

8 Bake until a skewer inserted into the centre comes out clean, 50–60 minutes. Leave to stand for 10 minutes before transferring to a rack.

Dried Fruit Loaf

MAKES 1 LOAF

450g/1lb/2²/₃ cups mixed dried fruit, such as currants, raisins, chopped ready-to-eat dried apricots and dried cherries

300ml/¹/₂ pint/1¹/₄ cups cold strong tea

200g/7oz/scant 1 cup soft dark brown sugar

grated rind and juice of 1 small orange

grated rind and juice of 1 lemon

1 egg, lightly beaten

200g/7oz/1³/₄ cups plain (all-purpose) flour

15ml/1 tbsp baking powder

pinch of salt

1 ▲ In a bowl, mix the dried fruit with the tea and soak overnight.

2 Preheat the oven to 180°C/350°F/Gas 4. Line the base and sides of a 23 × 13cm/9 × 5in loaf tin (pan) with baking parchment and grease the paper.

3 ▲ Strain the fruit, reserving the liquid. In a bowl, combine the brown sugar, grated orange and lemon rind, and fruit.

4 ▼ Pour the orange and lemon juice into a measuring jug (cup); if the quantity is less than 250ml/8fl oz/1 cup, top up with the soaking liquid.

5 Stir the citrus juices and egg into the dried fruit mixture.

6 In another bowl, sift together the flour, baking powder and salt. Stir into the fruit mixture until blended.

7 Transfer to the prepared tin and bake until a skewer inserted into the centre comes out clean, about 1¹/₄ hours. Leave to stand for 10 minutes before turning out.

Bilberry Tea Bread

MAKES 8 PIECES

50g/2oz/¼ cup butter or margarine, at room temperature

175g/6oz/scant 1 cup caster (superfine) sugar

1 egg, at room temperature

120ml/4fl oz/½ cup milk

225g/8oz/2 cups plain (all-purpose) flour

10ml/2 tsp baking powder

2.5ml/½ tsp salt

275g/10oz/2½ cups fresh bilberries, or blueberries

FOR THE TOPPING

115g/4oz/generous ½ cup sugar

40g/1½oz/⅓ cup plain (all-purpose) flour

2.5ml/½ tsp ground cinnamon

50g/2oz/¼ cup butter, cut in pieces

1 Preheat the oven to 190°C/375°F/ Gas 5. Grease a 23cm/9in baking dish.

2 With an electric mixer, cream the butter or margarine with the sugar until light and fluffy. Add the egg, beat to combine, then mix in the milk until blended.

3 ▼ Sift over the flour, baking powder and salt, and stir just enough to blend the ingredients.

4 ▲ Add the berries and stir.

5 Transfer to the baking dish.

6 ▲ For the topping, place the sugar, flour, cinnamon and butter into a mixing bowl. Cut in with a pastry blender until the mixture resembles coarse breadcrumbs.

7 ▲ Sprinkle the topping over the mixture in the baking dish.

8 Bake until a skewer inserted into the centre comes out clean, about 45 minutes. Serve warm or cold.

Chocolate Chip Walnut Loaf

MAKES 1 LOAF

90g/3¹/₂oz/¹/₂ cup caster (superfine) sugar

90g/3¹/₂oz/³/₄ cup plain (all-purpose) flour

5ml/1 tsp baking powder

60ml/4 tbsp cornflour (cornstarch)

130g/4 ¹/₂oz/generous ¹/₂ cup butter, at room temperature

2 eggs, at room temperature

5ml/1 tsp vanilla extract

30ml/2 tbsp currants or raisins

25g/1oz/¹/₄ cup walnuts, finely chopped

grated rind of ¹/₂ lemon

45ml/3 tbsp plain (semisweet) chocolate chips

icing (confectioners') sugar, for dusting

1 Preheat the oven to 180°C/350°F/ Gas 4. Grease and line a 21 × 12cm/ 8¹/₂ × 4¹/₂in loaf tin (pan).

2 ▲ Sprinkle 25ml/1¹/₂ tbsp of the caster sugar into the pan and tilt to distribute the sugar in an even layer over the base and sides. Shake out any excess.

~ VARIATION ~

For the best results, the eggs should be at room temperature. If they are too cold when folded into the creamed butter mixture, they may separate. If this happens, add a spoonful of the flour to help stabilize the mixture.

3 ▼ Sift together the flour, baking powder and cornflour into a mixing bowl, three times. Set aside.

4 With an electric mixer, cream the butter until soft. Add the remaining sugar and continue beating until light and fluffy. Add the eggs, one at a time, beating to incorporate thoroughly after each addition.

5 Gently fold the dry ingredients into the butter mixture, in three batches; do not overmix.

6 ▲ Fold in the vanilla, currants or raisins, walnuts, lemon rind, and chocolate chips until just blended.

7 Pour the mixture into the prepared tin and bake until a skewer inserted into the centre comes out clean, 45–50 minutes. Leave to cool in the tin for 5 minutes before transferring to a rack to cool completely. Dust over an even layer of icing sugar before serving.

Glazed Banana Spice Loaf

Makes 1 loaf

1 large ripe banana
115g/4oz/$^{1}/_{2}$ cup butter, at room temperature
165g/5$^{1}/_{2}$oz/generous $^{3}/_{4}$ cup caster (superfine) sugar
2 eggs, at room temperature
215g/7$^{1}/_{2}$ oz/scant 2 cups plain (all-purpose) flour
5ml/1 tsp salt
5ml/1 tsp bicarbonate of soda (baking soda)
2.5ml/$^{1}/_{2}$ tsp freshly grated nutmeg
1.5ml/$^{1}/_{4}$ tsp ground allspice
1.5ml/$^{1}/_{4}$ tsp ground cloves
175ml/6fl oz/$^{3}/_{4}$ cup sour cream
5ml/1 tsp vanilla extract
For the glaze
115g/4oz/1 cup icing (confectioners') sugar
15–30ml/1–2 tbsp lemon juice

1 Preheat the oven to 180°C/350°F/ Gas 4. Line a 21 × 11cm/8$^{1}/_{2}$ × 4$^{1}/_{2}$in loaf tin (pan) with baking parchment; grease.

2 ▼ With a fork, mash the banana in a bowl. Set aside.

3 With an electric mixer, cream the butter and sugar until light and fluffy. Add the eggs, one at a time, beating to blend well after each addition.

4 Sift together the flour, salt, bicarbonate of soda, nutmeg, allspice and cloves. Add to the butter mixture and stir to combine well.

5 ▲ Add the sour cream, banana, and vanilla and mix just enough to blend. Pour into the prepared tin.

6 ▲ Bake until the top springs back when touched lightly, 45–50 minutes. Leave to cool in the pan for 10 minutes. Turn out on to a wire rack to cool.

7 ▲ For the glaze, combine the icing sugar and lemon juice, then stir until smooth.

8 To glaze, place the cooled loaf on a rack set over a baking sheet. Pour the glaze over the top of the loaf and allow to set.

Sweet Sesame Loaf

MAKES 1 OR 2 LOAVES

75g/3oz/6 tbsp sesame seeds
275g/10oz/2¹/₂ cups plain (all-purpose) flour
5ml/1 tsp salt
12.5ml/2¹/₂ tsp baking powder
50g/2oz/¹/₄ cup butter or margarine, at room temperature
130g/4¹/₂oz/scant ³/₄ cup sugar
2 eggs, at room temperature
grated rind of 1 lemon
350ml/12fl oz/1¹/₂ cups milk

1 Preheat the oven to 180°C/350°F/ Gas 4. Line a 23 × 13cm/9 × 5in loaf tin (pan) with baking parchment and grease.

2 ▲ Reserve 30ml/2 tbsp of the sesame seeds. Spread the remainder on a baking sheet and bake until lightly toasted, about 10 minutes.

3 Sift the flour, salt and baking powder into a bowl.

4 ▲ Stir in the toasted sesame seeds and set aside.

5 With an electric mixer, cream the butter or margarine and sugar together until light and fluffy. Beat in the eggs, then stir in the lemon rind and milk.

6 ▼ Pour the milk mixture over the dry ingredients and fold in with a large metal spoon until just blended.

7 ▲ Pour into the tin and sprinkle over the reserved sesame seeds.

8 Bake until a skewer inserted into the centre comes out clean, about 1 hour. Leave to cool in the tin for about 10 minutes. Turn out on to a wire rack to cool completely.

Wholemeal Scones

MAKES 16

175g/6oz/³/4 cup cold butter

350g/12oz/3 cups wholemeal (whole-wheat) flour

150g/5oz/1¹/4 cups plain (all-purpose) flour

30ml/2 tbsp caster (superfine) sugar

2.5ml/¹/2 tsp salt

12.5ml/2¹/2 tsp bicarbonate of soda (baking soda)

2 eggs

175ml/6fl oz/³/4 cup buttermilk

35g/1¹/4oz/2¹/2 tbsp raisins

1 Preheat the oven to 200°C/400°F/ Gas 6. Grease and flour a large baking sheet.

2 ▲ Cut the butter into small pieces.

3 Combine the dry ingredients in a bowl. Add the butter and rub in with your fingertips until the mixture resembles coarse breadcrumbs. Set aside.

4 In another bowl, whisk together the eggs and buttermilk. Set aside 30ml/2 tbsp for glazing.

5 Stir the remaining egg mixture into the dry ingredients until it just holds together. Stir in the raisins.

6 Roll out the dough to about 2cm/ ³/4in thick. Stamp out circles with a biscuit (cookie) cutter. Place on the prepared sheet and brush with the glaze.

7 Bake until golden, 12–15 minutes. Allow to cool slightly before serving. Split in two with a fork while still warm and spread with butter and jam, if you like.

Orange and Raisin Scones

MAKES 16

275g/10oz/2¹/2 cups plain (all-purpose) flour

7.5ml/1¹/2 tsp baking powder

60g/2¹/4oz/4¹/2 tbsp sugar

2.5ml/¹/2 tsp salt

65g/2¹/2oz/5 tbsp butter, diced

65g/2¹/2oz/5 tbsp margarine, diced

grated rind of 1 large orange

50g/2oz/4 tbsp raisins

120ml/4fl oz/¹/2 cup buttermilk

milk, for glazing

1 Preheat the oven to 220°C/425°F/ Gas 7. Grease and flour a large baking sheet.

2 Combine the dry ingredients in a large bowl. Add the butter and margarine and rub in with your fingertips until the mixture resembles coarse breadcrumbs.

3 ▲ Add the orange rind and raisins.

4 Gradually stir in the buttermilk to form a soft dough.

5 ▲ Roll out the dough to about 2cm/³/4in thick. Stamp out circles with a biscuit (cookie) cutter.

6 ▲ Place on the prepared sheet and brush the tops with milk.

7 Bake until golden, 12–15 minutes. Serve hot or warm, with butter, or whipped or clotted cream, and jam.

~ COOK'S TIP ~

For light, tender scones, handle the dough as little as possible. If you wish, split the scones when cool and toast them under a preheated grill (broiler). Butter them while still hot.

Wholemeal Scones (top), Orange and Raisin Scones

Buttermilk Scones

MAKES 15

200g/7oz/1³/₄ cups plain (all-purpose) flour

5ml/1 tsp salt

5ml/1 tsp baking powder

2.5ml/¹/₂ tsp bicarbonate of soda (baking soda)

60ml/4 tbsp cold butter or margarine

175ml/6fl oz/³/₄ cup buttermilk

1 Preheat the oven to 220°C/425°F/ Gas 7. Grease and flour a baking sheet.

2 Sift the dry ingredients into a bowl. Rub in the butter or margarine with your fingertips until the mixture resembles breadcrumbs.

3 ▼ Gradually pour in the buttermilk, stirring with a fork to form a soft dough.

4 ▲ Roll out the dough to about 1cm/¹/₂in thick. Stamp out rounds with a 5cm/2in biscuit (cookie) cutter.

5 Place on the prepared baking sheet and bake until golden, 12–15 minutes. Serve warm or at room temperature.

Traditional Sweet Scones

MAKES 8

175g/6oz/1¹/₂ cups plain (all-purpose) flour

30ml/2 tbsp sugar

15ml/1 tbsp baking powder

pinch of salt

75ml/5 tbsp cold butter, cut in pieces

120ml/4fl oz/¹/₂ cup milk

1 Preheat the oven to 220°C/425°F/ Gas 7. Grease and flour a baking sheet.

2 ▲ Sift the flour, sugar, baking powder, and salt into a bowl.

3 Cut in the butter with a pastry blender until the mixture resembles coarse crumbs.

4 Pour in the milk and stir with a fork to form a soft dough.

> **~ VARIATION ~**
>
> To make a delicious and speedy dessert, split the scones in half while still warm. Butter one half, top with lightly sugared fresh strawberries, raspberries or blueberries, and sandwich with the other half. Serve at once with dollops of whipped cream.

5 ▲ Roll out the dough to about 5mm/¹/₄in thick. Stamp out rounds using a 6cm/2¹/₂in biscuit (cookie) cutter.

6 Place on the prepared sheet and bake until golden, about 12 minutes. Serve hot or warm, with butter and jam, to accompany tea or coffee.

Buttermilk Scones (top), Traditional Sweet Scones

Herb Popovers

MAKES 12

3 eggs

250ml/8fl oz/1 cup milk

25g/1oz/2 tbsp butter, melted

75g/3oz/⅔ cup plain (all-purpose) flour

pinch of salt

1 small sprig each mixed fresh herbs, such as chives, tarragon, dill and parsley

1 Preheat the oven to 220°C/425°F/Gas 7. Grease 12 small ramekins or individual baking cups.

2 With an electric mixer, beat the eggs until blended. Beat in the milk and melted butter.

3 Sift together the flour and salt, then beat into the egg mixture to combine thoroughly.

4 ▼ Strip the herb leaves from the stems and chop finely. Mix together and measure out 30ml/2 tbsp. Stir the herbs into the batter.

5 ▲ Fill the prepared cups half-full.

6 Bake until golden, 25–30 minutes. Do not open the oven door during baking time or the popovers may collapse. For drier popovers, pierce each one with a knife after the 30 minute baking time and bake for 5 minutes more. Serve hot.

Cheese Popovers

MAKES 12

3 eggs

250ml/8fl oz/1 cup milk

25g/1oz/2 tbsp butter, melted

75g/3oz/⅔ cup plain (all-purpose) flour

1.5ml/¼ tsp salt

1.5ml/¼ tsp paprika

25g/1oz/⅓ cup freshly grated Parmesan cheese

~ VARIATION ~

For traditional Yorkshire Pudding, omit the cheese and paprika, and use 50–75g/2–3oz/4–6 tbsp of beef dripping to replace the butter. Put them into the oven in time to serve warm as an accompaniment for roast beef.

1 Preheat the oven to 220°C/425°F/Gas 7.

2 ▲ Grease 12 small ramekins or individual baking cups. With an electric mixer, beat the eggs until they are blended. Beat in the milk and melted butter.

3 ▲ Sift together the flour, salt and paprika, then beat into the egg mixture. Add the cheese and stir.

4 Fill the prepared cups half-full and bake until golden, 25–30 minutes. Do not open the oven door or the popovers may collapse. For drier popovers, pierce each one with a knife after the 30 minute baking time and bake for 5 minutes more. Serve hot.

Herb Popovers (top), Cheese Popovers

Country

MAKES 2 LOAVES

350g/12oz/3 cups whole
   (whole-wheat) flour

350g/12oz/3 cups plain

150g/5oz/1¼ cups stron

20ml/4 tsp salt

50g/2oz/¼ cup butter, at

475ml/16fl oz/2 cups luk

FOR THE STARTER

15ml/1 tbsp active dry y

250ml/8fl oz/1 cup luke

150g/5oz/1¼ cups stron

1.5ml/¼ tsp caster (sup

1 ▲ For the starter,
yeast, water, flour and
and stir with a fork. C
in a warm place for 2–
overnight in a cool pl

2 Place the flours, sal
food processor and pr
blended, 1–2 minutes

3 Stir together the m
then slowly pour into
with the motor runnin
mixture forms a dough
add more water. Alter
dough can be mixed b
to a floured surface an
smooth and elastic.

4 Place in an ungreas
with a plastic bag, and
a warm place until do
about 1½ hours.

YEAST BREADS

THOUGH THE PACE OF TODAY'S LIFE
LEAVES LITTLE TIME FOR BAKING,
BREADMAKING CAN BE VERY
THERAPEUTIC. THE PROCESS IS
SIMPLE YET INFINITELY VARIABLE,
AS THE LOAVES THAT FOLLOW
PROVE. ROLL UP YOUR SLEEVES AND
CREATE A TRADITION.

White

Braided Loaf

MAKES 2 LOAVES

50ml/2fl oz/¼ cup l

15ml/1 tbsp active

30ml/2 tbsp sugar

450ml/16fl oz/2 cup

25g/1oz/2 tbsp butter
   at room temperatu

10ml/2 tsp salt

850–900g/1lb 14oz–
   white bread flour

MAKES 1 LOAF

15ml/1 tbsp active dried yeast

5ml/1 tsp honey

250ml/8fl oz/1 cup lukewarm milk

50g/2oz/¼ cup butter, melted

425g/15oz/3½ cups strong white
   bread flour

5ml/1 tsp salt

1 egg, lightly beaten

1 egg yolk beaten with 5ml/1 tsp milk,
   for glazing

1 ▼ Combine the yeast, honey, milk and butter. Stir and leave for 15 minutes to dissolve.

1 Combine the w
15ml/1 tbsp of sug
cup and leave to s
until the mixture

2 In a large bowl, mix together the flour and salt. Make a well in the centre and add the yeast mixture and egg. With a wooden spoon, stir from the centre, incorporating flour with each turn, to obtain a rough dough.

3 Transfer to a floured surface and knead until smooth and elastic. Place in a clean bowl, cover and leave to rise in a warm place until doubled in volume, about 1½ hours.

4 Grease a baking sheet. Knock back (punch down) the dough and divide into three equal pieces. Roll to shape each piece into a long, thin strip.

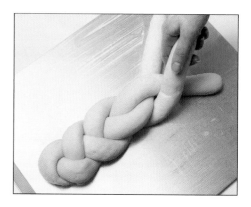

5 ▲ Begin braiding with the centre strip, tucking in the ends. Cover loosely and leave to rise in a warm place for 30 minutes.

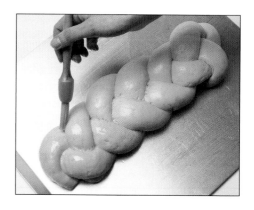

6 ▲ Preheat the oven to 190°C/ 375°F/Gas 5. Place the bread in a cool place while the oven heats. Brush with the glaze and bake until golden, 40–45 minutes. Turn out on to a rack to cool.

Sesame Seed Bread

MAKES 1 LOAF

10ml/2 tsp active dried yeast
300ml/½ pint/1¼ cups lukewarm water
200g/7oz/1¾ cups strong white bread flour
200g/7oz/1¾ cups strong wholemeal (whole-wheat) bread flour
10ml/2 tsp salt
65g/2½oz/5 tbsp toasted sesame seeds
milk, for glazing
25g/1oz/2 tbsp sesame seeds, for sprinkling

1 Combine the yeast and 75ml/5 tbsp of the water and leave to dissolve for 15 minutes. Mix the flours and salt in a large bowl. Make a well in the centre and pour in the yeast and water.

2 ▲ With a wooden spoon, stir from the centre, incorporating flour with each turn, to obtain a rough dough.

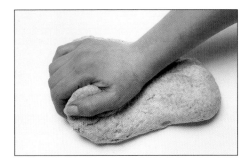

3 ▲ Transfer to a lightly floured surface. To knead, push the dough away from you with the palm of your hand, then fold it towards you and push away again. Repeat until smooth and elastic, then return to the bowl and cover with a plastic bag. Leave the dough in a warm place for about 1½–2 hours, until doubled in volume.

4 ▲ Grease a 23cm/9in cake tin (pan). Knock back (punch down) the dough and knead in the sesame seeds. Divide the dough into 16 balls and place in the tin. Cover with a plastic bag and leave in a warm place until risen above the rim of the tin.

5 ▼ Preheat the oven to 220°C/425°F/Gas 7. Brush the loaf with milk and sprinkle with the sesame seeds. Bake for 15 minutes. Lower the heat to 190°C/375°F/Gas 5 and bake until the bottom sounds hollow when tapped, about 30 minutes. Cool on a rack.

Wholemeal Bread

MAKES 1 LOAF

600g/1lb 5oz/5¼ cups strong wholemeal (whole-wheat) bread flour

10ml/2 tsp salt

20ml/4 tsp active dried yeast

425ml/15fl oz/generous 1⅔ cups lukewarm water

30ml/2 tbsp honey

45ml/3 tbsp oil

40g/1½oz wheatgerm

milk, for glazing

1 Combine the flour and salt in a bowl and place in the oven at its lowest setting until warmed, 8–10 minutes.

2 Meanwhile, combine the yeast with half of the water in a small bowl and leave to dissolve.

3 ▼ Make a well in the centre of the flour. Pour in the yeast mixture, the remaining water, honey, oil and wheatgerm. With a wooden spoon, stir from the centre until smooth.

4 Transfer the dough to a lightly floured surface and knead just enough to shape into a loaf.

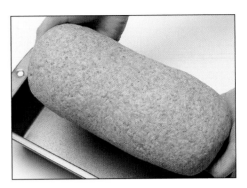

5 ▲ Grease a 23 × 13cm/9 × 5in loaf tin (pan), place the dough in it and cover with a plastic bag. Leave in a warm place until the dough is about 2.5cm/1in higher than the tin rim, about 1 hour.

6 Preheat the oven to 200°C/400°F/ Gas 6. Bake until the bottom sounds hollow when tapped, 35–40 minutes. Cool.

Rye Bread

MAKES 1 LOAF

200g/7oz/1¾ cups rye flour

450ml/¾ pint/scant 2 cups boiling water

120ml/4fl oz/½ cup black treacle (molasses)

65g/2½oz/5 tbsp butter, cut in pieces

15ml/1 tbsp salt

30ml/2 tbsp caraway seeds

15ml/1 tbsp active dried yeast

120ml/4fl oz/½ cup lukewarm water

about 850g/1lb 14oz/7½ cups strong white bread flour

semolina or flour, for dusting

1 ▲ Mix the rye flour, boiling water, treacle, butter, salt and caraway seeds in a large bowl. Leave to cool.

2 In another bowl, mix the yeast and lukewarm water and leave to dissolve. Stir into the rye flour mixture. Stir in just enough strong flour to obtain a stiff dough. If it becomes too stiff, stir with your hands.

3 Transfer to a floured surface and knead until the dough is no longer sticky and is smooth and shiny.

4 Place in a greased bowl, cover with a plastic bag, and leave in a warm place until doubled in volume. Knock back (punch down) the dough, cover, and leave to rise again for 30 minutes.

5 Preheat the oven to 180°C/350°F/ Gas 4. Dust a baking sheet with semolina.

6 ▼ Shape the dough into a ball. Place on the sheet and score several times across the top. Bake until the bottom sounds hollow when tapped, about 40 minutes. Cool on a rack.

~ COOK'S TIP ~

To bring out the flavour of the caraway seeds, toast them lightly. Spread the seeds on a baking tray and place in a preheated 160°C/325°F/ Gas 3 oven for about 7 minutes.

Wholemeal Bread (top), Rye Bread

Buttermilk Graham Bread

MAKES 8

10ml/2 tsp active dried yeast

120ml/4fl oz/¹/₂ cup lukewarm water

225g/8oz/2 cups graham or strong
    wholemeal (whole-wheat)
    bread flour

350g/12oz/3 cups strong white
    bread flour

130g/4¹/₂oz/generous 1 cup cornmeal

10ml/2 tsp salt

30ml/2 tbsp sugar

60ml/4 tbsp butter, at room temperature

475ml/16fl oz/2 cups lukewarm buttermilk

1 beaten egg, for glazing

sesame seeds, for sprinkling

1 Combine the yeast and water, stir, and leave for 15 minutes to dissolve.

2 ▲ Mix together the two flours, cornmeal, salt and sugar in a large bowl. Make a well in the centre and pour in the yeast mixture, then add the butter and the buttermilk.

3 ▲ Stir from the centre, mixing in the flour until a rough dough is formed. If too stiff, use your hands.

4 ▲ Transfer to a floured surface and knead until smooth. Place in a clean bowl, cover, and leave in a warm place for 2–3 hours.

5 ▲ Grease two 20cm/8in square baking tins (pans). Knock back (punch down) the dough. Divide into eight pieces and roll them into balls. Place four in each tin. Cover and leave in a warm place for about 1 hour.

6 Preheat the oven to 190°C/375°F/ Gas 5. Brush with the glaze, then sprinkle over the sesame seeds. Bake for about 50 minutes, or until the bottoms sound hollow when tapped. Cool on a wire rack.

Multi-grain Bread

MAKES 2 LOAVES

15ml/1 tbsp active dried yeast

50ml/2fl oz/¼ cup lukewarm water

65g/2½oz/⅔ cup rolled oats (not quick cook)

450ml/¾ pint/scant 2 cups milk

10ml/2 tsp salt

50ml/2fl oz/¼ cup oil

50g/2oz/¼ cup soft light brown sugar

30ml/2 tbsp honey

2 eggs, lightly beaten

25g/1oz wheatgerm

175g/6oz/1½ cups soya flour

350g/12oz/3 cups strong wholemeal (whole-wheat) bread flour

about 450g/1lb/4 cups strong white bread flour

1 Combine the yeast and water, stir, and leave for 15 minutes to dissolve.

2 ▲ Place the oats in a large bowl. Scald the milk, then pour over the rolled oats.

3 Stir in the salt, oil, sugar and honey. Leave until lukewarm.

~ VARIATION ~

Different flours may be used in this recipe, such as rye, barley, buckwheat or cornmeal. Try replacing the wheatgerm and the soya flour with one or two of these, using the same total amount.

4 ▲ Stir in the yeast mixture, eggs, wheatgerm, soya and wholemeal flours. Gradually stir in enough white flour to obtain a rough dough.

5 Transfer the dough to a floured surface and knead, adding flour if necessary, until smooth and elastic. Return to a clean bowl, cover and leave to rise in a warm place until doubled in volume, about 2½ hours.

6 Grease two 21 × 12cm/8½ × 4½in bread tins (pans). Knock back (punch down) the risen dough and knead briefly.

7 Divide the dough into quarters. Roll each quarter into a cylinder 4cm/1½in thick. Twist together 2 cylinders and put in a tin; repeat for the remaining pieces.

8 Cover and leave to rise until doubled in size, about 1 hour.

9 Preheat the oven to 190°C/375°F/Gas 5.

10 ▲ Bake for 45–50 minutes, until the bottoms sound hollow when tapped lightly. Cool on a rack.

Potato Bread

MAKES 2 LOAVES

20ml/4 tsp active dried yeast

250ml/8fl oz/1 cup lukewarm milk

225g/8oz potatoes, boiled (reserve 250ml/ 8fl oz/1 cup of potato cooking liquid)

30ml/2 tbsp oil

20ml/4 tsp salt

850–900g/1lb 14oz–2lb/7½–8 cups strong white bread flour

1 Combine the yeast and milk in a large bowl and leave to dissolve, about 15 minutes.

2 Meanwhile, mash the potatoes.

3 ▲ Add the potatoes, oil and salt to the yeast mixture and mix well. Stir in the reserved cooking water, then stir in the flour, in six separate batches, to form a stiff dough.

4 Transfer to a floured surface and knead until smooth and elastic. Return to the bowl, cover, and leave in a warm place until doubled in size, 1–1½ hours. Knock back (punch down), then leave to rise for another 40 minutes.

5 Grease two 23 × 13cm/9 × 5in loaf tins (pans). Roll the dough into 20 small balls. Place two rows of balls in each tin. Leave until the dough has risen above the rim of the tins.

6 Preheat the oven to 200°C/400°F/ Gas 6. Bake for 10 minutes, then lower the heat to 190°C/375°F/Gas 5. Bake until the bottoms sound hollow when tapped, 40 minutes. Cool on a rack.

Irish Soda Bread

MAKES 1 LOAF

275g/10oz/2½ cups plain (all-purpose) flour

150g/5oz/1¼ cups wholemeal (whole-wheat) flour

5ml/1 tsp bicarbonate of soda (baking soda)

5ml/1 tsp salt

25g/1oz/2 tbsp butter or margarine, at room temperature

300ml/½ pint/1¼ cups buttermilk

15ml/1 tbsp plain flour, for dusting

1 Preheat the oven to 200°C/400°F/ Gas 6. Grease a baking sheet.

2 Sift the flours, bicarbonate of soda and salt together into a bowl. Make a well in the centre and add the butter or margarine and buttermilk. Working outwards from the centre, stir with a fork until a soft dough is formed.

3 ▲ With floured hands, gather the dough into a ball.

4 ▲ Transfer to a floured surface and knead for 3 minutes. Shape the dough into a large round.

5 ▲ Place on the baking sheet. Cut a cross in the top with a sharp knife.

6 ▲ Dust with flour. Bake until brown, 40–50 minutes. Transfer to a rack to cool.

Potato Bread (top), Irish Soda Bread

Anadama Bread

MAKES 2 LOAVES

10ml/2 tsp active dried yeast
60ml/4 tbsp lukewarm water
50g/2oz/^{1}/$_2$ cup cornmeal
45ml/3 tbsp butter or margarine
60ml/4 tbsp black treacle (molasses)
175ml/6fl oz/^{3}/$_4$ cup boiling water
1 egg
350g/12oz/3 cups strong white bread flour
30ml/2 tbsp salt

1 Combine the yeast and lukewarm water, stir well, and leave for 15 minutes to dissolve.

2 ▼ Meanwhile, combine the cornmeal, butter or margarine, black treacle and boiling water in a large bowl. Add the yeast, egg, and half the flour. Stir together to blend.

3 ▲ Stir in the remaining flour and salt. When the dough becomes too stiff, stir with your hands until it comes away from the sides of the bowl. If it is too sticky, add more flour; if too stiff, add a little water.

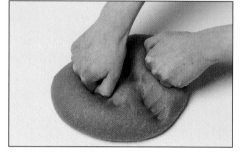

4 ▲ Transfer to a floured surface and knead until smooth and elastic. Place in a bowl, cover with a plastic bag, and leave in a warm place until doubled in size, 2–3 hours.

5 Grease two 18 × 7.5cm/7 × 3in bread tins (pans). Knock back (punch down) the dough. Shape into two loaves and place in the tins, seam-side down. Cover and leave in a warm place for 1–2 hours.

6 ▲ Preheat the oven to 190°C/ 375°F/Gas 5. Bake for 50 minutes. Remove and cool on a wire rack.

Oatmeal Bread

MAKES 2 LOAVES

450ml/³/₄ pint/scant 2 cups milk
25g/1oz/2 tbsp butter
50g/2oz/¹/₄ cup soft dark brown sugar
10ml/2 tsp salt
15ml/1 tbsp active dried yeast
50ml/2fl oz/¹/₄ cup lukewarm water
400g/14oz/4 cups rolled oats (not quick-cook)
700–850g/1¹/₂lb–1lb 14oz/6–7¹/₂ cups strong white bread flour

1 ▲ Scald the milk. Remove from the heat and stir in the butter, brown sugar and salt. Leave until lukewarm.

2 Combine the yeast and warm water in a large bowl and leave until the yeast is dissolved and the mixture is frothy. Stir in the milk mixture.

3 ▲ Add 270g/10oz/2¹/₄ cups of the oats and enough flour to obtain a soft dough.

4 Transfer to a floured surface and knead until smooth and elastic.

5 ▲ Place in a greased bowl, cover with a plastic bag, and leave until doubled in volume, 2–3 hours.

6 Grease a large baking sheet. Transfer the dough to a lightly floured surface and divide in half.

7 ▼ Shape into rounds. Place on the baking sheet, cover with a dish towel and leave to rise until doubled in volume, about 1 hour.

8 Preheat the oven to 200°C/400°F/ Gas 6. Score the tops and sprinkle with the remaining oats. Bake until the bottoms sound hollow when tapped, 45–50 minutes. Cool on racks.

Sourdough Bread

MAKES 1 LOAF

350g/12oz/3 cups strong white bread flour

15ml/1 tbsp salt

250ml/8fl oz/1 cup Sourdough Starter

120ml/4fl oz/½ cup lukewarm water

1 ▲ Combine the flour and salt in a large bowl. Make a well in the centre and add the starter and water. With a wooden spoon, stir from the centre, incorporating more flour with each turn, to obtain a rough dough.

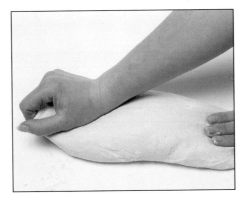

2 ▲ Transfer the dough to a floured surface. To knead, push the dough away from you with the palm of your hand, then fold it towards you, and push it away again. Repeat the process until the dough has become smooth and elastic.

3 Place in a clean bowl, cover, and leave to rise in a warm place until doubled in volume, for about 2 hours.

4 Lightly grease a 20 × 10cm/8 × 4in bread tin (pan).

5 ▼ Knock back (punch down) the dough with your fist. Knead briefly, then form into a loaf shape and place in the tin, seam-side down. Cover with a plastic bag, and leave to rise in a warm place, for about 1½ hours.

6 Preheat the oven to 220°C/425°F/Gas 7. Dust the top of the loaf with flour, then score lengthways. Bake for 15 minutes. Lower the heat to 190°C/375°F/Gas 5 and bake for about 30 minutes more, or until the bottom sounds hollow when tapped.

Sourdough Starter

MAKES 750ML/1¼ PINTS

5ml/1 tsp active dried yeast

175ml/6fl oz/¾ cup lukewarm water

50g/2oz/½ cup strong white bread flour

~ COOK'S TIP ~

After using, feed the remaining starter with a handful of flour and enough water to restore it to a thick batter. The starter can be chilled for up to 1 week, but must be brought back to room temperature before using.

1 ▲ Combine the yeast and water, stir and leave for 15 minutes to dissolve.

2 ▼ Sprinkle over the flour, and whisk until it forms a batter. Cover and leave to rise in a warm place for at least 24 hours or preferably 2–4 days, before using.

Sourdough French Loaves

MAKES 2 LOAVES

10ml/2 tsp active dried yeast
350ml/12fl oz/1½ cups lukewarm water
250ml/8fl oz/1 cup Sourdough Starter
700g/1lb 8oz/6 cups strong white bread flour
15ml/1 tbsp salt
5ml/1 tsp sugar
cornmeal, for sprinkling
5ml/1 tsp cornflour (cornstarch)
120ml/4fl oz/½ cup water

1 In a large bowl, combine the yeast and lukewarm water, stir and leave for 15 minutes to dissolve.

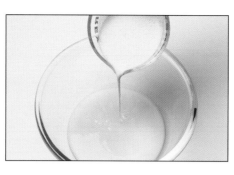

2 ▲ Pour in the Sourdough Starter. Add 450g/1lb/4 cups of the flour, the salt and the sugar. Stir until smooth. Cover the bowl with a plastic bag and leave the dough to rise in a warm place until doubled in volume, about 1½ hours.

3 Stir in just enough flour to obtain a rough dough. Transfer to a floured surface and knead until the dough is smooth and elastic. Divide in half, then shape each half into a 35cm/14in cylinder with rounded ends.

4 ▲ Place the loaves on a wooden board or tray sprinkled with cornmeal. Cover loosely with a dishtowel and leave to rise in a warm place until nearly doubled in volume.

5 Preheat the oven to 220°C/425°F/ Gas 7. Place a 38 × 30cm/15 × 12in baking sheet in the oven. Half-fill a shallow baking dish with hot water and put it on the bottom of the oven.

6 Mix the cornflour and water in a small pan. Bring to the boil.

7 ▲ With a sharp knife, make several diagonal slashes across the loaves. Slide on to the hot baking sheet and brush over the cornflour mixture. Bake until the tops are golden and the bottoms sound hollow when tapped, about 25 minutes. Cool on a wire rack.

Sourdough Rye Bread

MAKES 2 LOAVES

10ml/2 tsp active dried yeast
120ml/4fl oz/$^1/_2$ cup lukewarm water
25g/1oz/2 tbsp butter, melted
15ml/1 tbsp salt
115g/4oz/1 cup strong wholemeal (whole-wheat) bread flour
400–450g/14–16oz/3$^1/_2$–4 cups strong white bread flour
1 egg mixed with 15ml/1 tbsp water, for glazing
FOR THE STARTER
15ml/1 tbsp active dried yeast
350ml/12fl oz/1$^1/_2$ cups lukewarm water
45ml/3 tbsp black treacle (molasses)
30ml/2 tbsp caraway seeds
250g/9oz/2$^1/_4$ cups rye flour

1 For the starter, combine the yeast and water, stir and leave for 15 minutes to dissolve.

2 ▲ Stir in the black treacle, caraway seeds and rye flour. Cover and leave in a warm place for 2–3 days.

3 In a large bowl, combine the yeast and water, stir and leave for 10 minutes. Stir in the melted butter, salt, wholemeal flour and 400g/14oz/3$^1/_2$ cups of the white flour.

4 ▲ Make a well in the centre and pour in the starter.

5 Stir to obtain a rough dough, then transfer to a floured surface and knead until smooth and elastic. Return to the bowl, cover and leave to rise in a warm place until doubled in volume, about 2 hours.

6 Grease a large baking sheet. Knock back (punch down) the dough and knead briefly. Cut the dough in half and form each half into log-shaped loaves.

7 ▼ Place the loaves on the baking sheet and score the tops with a sharp knife. Cover and leave to rise in a warm place until almost doubled, about 50 minutes.

8 Preheat the oven to 190°C/375°F/ Gas 5. Brush the loaves with the egg wash to glaze them, then bake until the bottoms sound hollow when tapped, about 50–55 minutes. If the tops brown too quickly, place a sheet of foil over the tops to protect them. Cool on a wire rack.

Wholemeal Rolls

MAKES 12

10ml/2 tsp active dried yeast

50ml/2fl oz/¼ cup lukewarm water

5ml/1 tsp caster (superfine) sugar

175ml/6fl oz/¾ cup lukewarm buttermilk

1.5ml/¼ tsp bicarbonate of soda
(baking soda)

5ml/1 tsp salt

40g/1½oz/3 tbsp butter,
at room temperature

200g/7oz/1¾ cups strong wholemeal
(whole-wheat) bread flour

150g/5oz/1¼ cups strong white
bread flour

1 beaten egg, for glazing

1 In a large bowl, combine the yeast,
water and sugar. Stir, and leave for
15 minutes to dissolve.

2 ▲ Add the buttermilk, bicarbonate
of soda, salt and butter, and stir to
blend. Stir in the wholemeal flour.

3 Add just enough of the white flour
to obtain a rough dough.

4 Transfer to a floured surface and
knead until smooth and elastic.
Divide into three equal parts.
Roll each into a cylinder, then cut
into four.

5 ▼ Form the pieces into torpedo
shapes. Place on a greased baking
sheet, cover and leave in a warm
place until doubled in volume.

6 Preheat the oven to 200°C/400°F/
Gas 6. Brush the rolls with the glaze.
Bake until firm, 15–20 minutes. Cool
on a rack.

French Bread

MAKES 2 LOAVES

15ml/1 tbsp active dried yeast

450ml/¾ pint/scant 2 cups lukewarm water

15ml/1 tbsp salt

850g–1.2kg/1lb 14oz–2½lb/7½–10 cups
strong white bread flour

semolina or flour, for sprinkling

1 Combine the yeast and water, stir,
and leave for 15 minutes to dissolve.
Stir in the salt.

2 Add the flour, 150g/5oz/1¼ cups at
a time. Beat in with a wooden spoon,
adding just enough flour to obtain a
smooth dough. Alternatively, use an
electric mixer with a dough hook.

3 Transfer to a floured surface and
knead until smooth and elastic.

4 Shape into a ball, place in a greased
bowl and cover with a plastic bag.
Leave to rise in a warm place until
doubled in volume, 2–4 hours.

5 ▲ Transfer to a lightly floured
board and shape into two long loaves.
Place on a baking sheet sprinkled with
semolina or flour and leave to rise for
5 minutes.

6 ▲ Score the tops in several places
with a very sharp knife. Brush with
water and place in a cold oven. Set a
pan of boiling water on the bottom of
the oven and set the oven to 200°C/
400°F/Gas 6. Bake until crusty and
golden, about 40 minutes. Cool
on a rack.

Wholemeal Rolls (top), French Bread

Pleated Rolls

MAKES 48

15ml/1 tbsp active dried yeast
475ml/16fl oz/2 cups lukewarm milk
115g/4oz/½ cup margarine
75ml/5 tbsp sugar
10ml/2 tsp salt
2 eggs
975g–1.2kg/2lb 3oz–2½lb/8⅔–10 cups strong white bread flour
50g/2oz/¼ cup butter

1 Combine the yeast and 120ml/ 4fl oz/½ cup milk in a large bowl. Stir and leave for 15 minutes to dissolve.

2 Scald the remaining milk, cool for 5 minutes, then beat in the margarine, sugar, salt and eggs. Leave to cool to lukewarm.

3 ▲ Pour the milk mixture into the yeast mixture. Stir in half the flour with a wooden spoon. Add the remaining flour, 150g/5oz/1¼ cups at a time, until a rough dough is obtained.

4 Transfer the dough to a lightly floured surface and knead until smooth and elastic. Place in a clean bowl, cover with a plastic bag and leave to rise in a warm place until doubled in volume, about 2 hours.

5 In a pan, melt the butter and set aside. Grease two baking sheets.

6 Knock back (punch down) the dough and divide into four equal pieces. Roll each piece into a 30 × 20cm/12 × 8in rectangle, about 5mm/¼in thick.

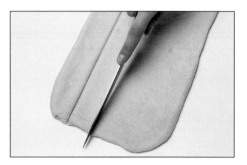

7 ▲ Cut each rectangle into four long strips. Cut each strip into three 10 × 5cm/4 × 2in rectangles.

8 ▲ Brush each rectangle with melted butter, then fold the rectangles in half, so that the top extends about 1cm/½in over the bottom.

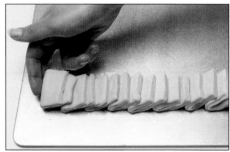

9 ▲ Place the rectangles slightly overlapping on the baking sheet, with the longer side facing up. Cover and chill for 30 minutes. Preheat the oven to 180°C/350°F/Gas 4. Bake until golden, about 18–20 minutes. Allow to cool slightly before slicing or breaking the rolls.

Clover Leaf Rolls

MAKES 24

300ml/¹/₂ pint/1¹/₄ cups milk

30ml/2 tbsp caster (superfine) sugar

50g/2oz/¹/₄ cup butter, at room temperature

10ml/2 tsp active dried yeast

1 egg

10ml/2 tsp salt

500–575g/1lb 2oz–1lb 4oz/4¹/₂–5 cups
   strong white bread flour

melted butter, for glazing

1 ▲ Heat the milk until lukewarm; test the temperature with your knuckle. Pour into a large bowl and stir in the sugar, butter and yeast. Leave for 15 minutes to dissolve.

2 Stir the egg and salt into the yeast mixture. Gradually stir in 500g/1lb 2oz/4¹/₂ cups of the flour. Add just enough extra flour to obtain a rough dough.

3 ▲ Transfer to a floured surface and knead until smooth and elastic. Place in a greased bowl, cover and leave in a warm place until doubled in volume, about 1¹/₂ hours.

4 Grease two 12-cup bun trays.

5 ▼ Knock back (punch down) the dough. Cut into four equal pieces. Roll each piece into a rope 35cm/14in long. Cut each rope into 18 pieces, then roll each into a ball.

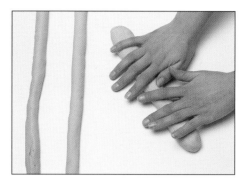

6 ▲ Place three balls, side by side, in each bun cup. Cover loosely and leave to rise in a warm place until doubled in volume, about 1¹/₂ hours.

7 Preheat the oven to 200°C/400°F/ Gas 6. Brush the rolls with glaze. Bake until lightly browned, about 20 minutes. Cool slightly before serving.

Poppyseed Knots

MAKES 12

300ml/¹/₂ pint/1¹/₄ cups lukewarm milk

50g/2oz/¹/₄ cup butter, at room temperature

5ml/1 tsp caster (superfine) sugar

10ml/2 tsp active dried yeast

1 egg yolk

10ml/2 tsp salt

500–575g/1lb 2oz–1lb 4oz/4¹/₂–5 cups
    strong white bread flour

1 egg beaten with 10ml/2 tsp of water,
    for glazing

poppyseeds, for sprinkling

1 In a large bowl, stir together the milk, butter, sugar and yeast. Leave for 15 minutes to dissolve.

2 Stir in the egg yolk, salt and 275g/10oz/2¹/₂ cups flour. Add half the remaining flour and stir to obtain a soft dough.

3 Transfer to a floured surface and knead, adding flour if necessary, until smooth and elastic. Place in a bowl, cover and leave in a warm place until doubled in volume, 1¹/₂–2 hours.

4 ▲ Grease a baking sheet. Knock back (punch down) the dough and cut into 12 pieces the size of golf balls.

5 ▲ Roll each piece to a rope, twist to form a knot and place 2.5cm/1in apart on the sheet. Cover and leave to rise until doubled in volume, 1–1¹/₂ hours.

6 Preheat the oven to 180°C/350°F/Gas 4.

7 ▲ Brush the knots with the egg glaze and sprinkle over the poppyseeds. Bake until the tops are lightly browned, 25–30 minutes. Cool slightly on a rack before serving.

Bread Sticks

MAKES 18–20

15ml/1 tbsp active dried yeast
300ml/¹/₂ pint/1¹/₄ cups lukewarm water
425g/15oz/3²/₃ cups strong white bread flour
10ml/2 tsp salt
5ml/1 tsp caster (superfine) sugar
30ml/2 tbsp olive oil
150g/5oz/10 tbsp sesame seeds
1 beaten egg, for glazing
coarse salt, for sprinkling

1 Combine the yeast and water, stir and leave for 15 minutes to dissolve.

2 ▲ Place the flour, salt, sugar and olive oil in a food processor. With the motor running, slowly pour in the yeast mixture, and process until the dough forms a ball. If sticky, add more flour; if dry, add more water.

3 Transfer to a floured surface and knead until smooth and elastic. Place in a bowl, cover and leave to rise in a warm place for 45 minutes.

4 ▲ Lightly toast the sesame seeds in a frying pan. Grease two baking sheets.

5 ▼ Roll small handfuls of dough into cylinders, about 30cm/12in long. Place on the baking sheets.

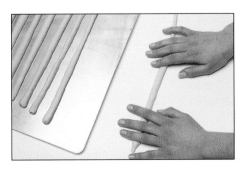

6 ▲ Brush with egg glaze, sprinkle with the sesame seeds, then sprinkle over some coarse salt. Leave to rise, uncovered, until almost doubled in volume, about 20 minutes.

7 Preheat the oven to 200°C/400°F/ Gas 6. Bake until golden, about 15 minutes. Turn off the heat but leave the bread sticks in the oven for 5 minutes more. Serve warm or cool.

~ VARIATION ~

If you like, use other seeds, such as poppy or caraway, or, for plain bread sticks, omit the seeds and salt.

Croissants

MAKES 18

15ml/1 tbsp active dried yeast
335ml/11fl oz/generous 1¼ cups lukewarm milk
10ml/2 tsp caster (superfine) sugar
7.5ml/1½ tsp salt
425–505g/15oz–1lb 2oz/3⅔–4½ cups strong white bread flour
225g/8oz/1 cup cold unsalted (sweet) butter
1 egg beaten with 10ml/2 tsp water, for glazing

1 Stir together the yeast and warm milk in a large bowl. Leave for 15 minutes to dissolve. Stir in the sugar, salt and 150g/5oz/1¼ cups of the flour.

2 Using a dough hook, on low speed, gradually add the remaining flour. Beat on high until the dough pulls away from the sides of the bowl. Cover and let rise in a warm place until doubled, about 1½ hours.

3 On a floured surface, knead the dough until smooth. Wrap it in baking parchment and chill for 15 minutes.

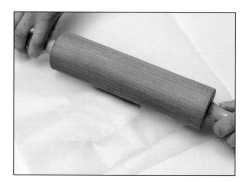

4 ▲ Divide the butter into two halves and place each between two sheets of baking parchment. With a rolling pin, flatten each to form a 15 × 10cm/6 × 4in rectangle. Set aside.

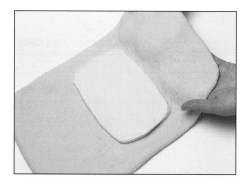

5 ▲ On a floured surface, roll out the dough to 30 × 20cm/12 × 8in. Place a butter rectangle in the centre. Fold the bottom third of dough over the butter and press gently to seal. Top with the other butter rectangle, then fold over the top dough third.

6 ▲ Turn the dough so that the short side is facing you, with the long folded edge on the left and the long open edge on the right, like a book.

7 Roll the dough gently into a 30 × 20cm/12 × 8in rectangle; do not press the butter out. Fold in thirds again and mark one corner with your fingertip to indicate the first turn. Wrap and chill for 30 minutes.

8 Repeat twice more: again position the dough like a book, roll, fold in thirds, mark, wrap, and chill. After the third fold, chill for at least 2 hours (or overnight).

9 Roll out the dough about 3mm/⅛in thick to a rectangle about 33cm/13in wide. Trim the sides to neaten.

10 ▲ Cut the dough in half lengthways, then cut into triangles 15cm/6in high with a 10cm/4in base.

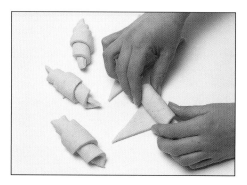

11 ▲ Gently go over the triangles lengthways with a rolling pin to stretch slightly. Roll up from base to point. Place point down on baking sheets and curve to form a crescent. Cover and leave to rise in a warm place until more than doubled in volume, 1–1½ hours. (Or, chill overnight and bake the next day.)

12 ▲ Preheat the oven to 240°C/ 475°F/Gas 9. Brush with the glaze. Bake for 2 minutes. Lower the heat to 190°C/375°F/Gas 5. Bake until golden, 10–12 more minutes. Serve warm.

Dill Bread

MAKES 2 LOAVES

20ml/4 tsp active dried yeast
475ml/16fl oz/2 cups lukewarm water
30ml/2 tbsp sugar
1.05kg/2lb 5¹/₂oz/9¹/₄ cups strong white bread flour
¹/₂ onion, chopped
60ml/4 tbsp oil
1 large bunch of dill, finely chopped
2 eggs, lightly beaten
165g/5¹/₂oz/¾ cup cottage cheese
20ml/4 tsp salt
milk, for glazing

1 Mix together the yeast, water and sugar in a large bowl and leave for 15 minutes to dissolve.

2 ▼ Stir in about half of the flour. Cover and leave to rise in a warm place for 45 minutes.

3 ▲ In a frying pan, cook the onion in 15ml/1 tbsp of the oil until soft. Set aside to cool, then stir into the yeast mixture. Stir the dill, eggs, cottage cheese, salt and remaining oil into the yeast. Gradually add the remaining flour until too stiff to stir.

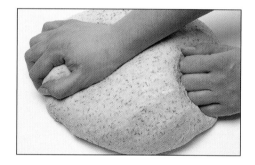

4 ▲ Transfer to a floured surface and knead until smooth and elastic. Place in a bowl, cover and leave to rise until doubled in volume, 1–1¹/₂ hours.

5 ▲ Grease a large baking sheet. Cut the dough in half and shape into two rounds. Leave to rise in a warm place for 30 minutes.

6 Preheat the oven to 190°C/375°F/Gas 5. Score the tops, brush with the milk and bake until browned, about 50 minutes. Cool on a rack.

Spiral Herb Bread

MAKES 2 LOAVES

30ml/2 tbsp active dried yeast
600ml/1 pint/2^1/$_2$ cups lukewarm water
425g/15oz/3^2/$_3$ cups strong white bread flour
505g/1lb 2oz/4^1/$_2$ cups strong wholemeal (whole-wheat) bread flour
15ml/3 tsp salt
25g/1oz/2 tbsp butter
1 large bunch of parsley, finely chopped
1 bunch of spring onions (scallions), chopped
1 garlic clove, finely chopped
salt and ground black pepper
1 egg, lightly beaten
milk, for glazing

1 Combine the yeast and 50ml/2fl oz/ ^{1}/$_4$ cup of the water, stir and leave for 15 minutes to dissolve.

2 Combine the flours and salt in a large bowl. Make a well in the centre and pour in the yeast mixture and the remaining water. With a wooden spoon, stir from the centre, working outwards to obtain a rough dough.

3 Transfer the dough to a floured surface and knead until smooth and elastic. Return to the bowl, cover with a plastic bag, and leave until doubled in volume, about 2 hours.

4 ▲ Meanwhile, combine the butter, parsley, spring onions and garlic in a large frying pan. Cook over low heat, stirring, until softened. Season and set aside.

5 Grease two 23 × 13cm/9 × 5in tins (pans). When the dough has risen, cut in half and roll each half into a rectangle about 35 × 23cm/14 × 9in.

6 ▼ Brush both with the beaten egg. Divide the herb mixture between the two, spreading just up to the edges.

7 ▲ Roll up to enclose the filling and pinch the short ends to seal. Place in the tins, seam-side down. Cover, and leave in a warm place until the dough rises above the rim of the tins.

8 Preheat the oven to 190°C/375°F/ Gas 5. Brush with milk and bake until the bottoms sound hollow when tapped, about 55 minutes. Cool on a rack.

Pizza

MAKES 2

505g/1lb 2oz/4¹⁄₂ cups strong white bread flour
5ml/1 tsp salt
10ml/2 tsp active dried yeast
300ml/¹⁄₂ pint/1¹⁄₄ cups lukewarm water
50–120ml/2–4fl oz/¹⁄₄–¹⁄₂ cup extra-virgin olive oil
tomato sauce, grated cheese, olives and herbs, for topping

1 Combine the flour and salt in a large mixing bowl. Make a well in the centre and add the yeast, water and 30ml/2 tbsp of the olive oil. Leave for 15 minutes to dissolve the yeast.

2 With your hands, stir until the dough just holds together. Transfer to a floured surface and knead until smooth and elastic. Avoid adding too much flour while kneading.

3 ▲ Brush the inside of a clean bowl with 15ml/1 tbsp of the oil. Place the dough in the bowl and roll around to coat with the oil. Cover with a plastic bag and leave to rise in a warm place until more than doubled in volume, about 45 minutes.

4 Divide the dough into two balls. Preheat the oven to 200°C/400°F/Gas 6.

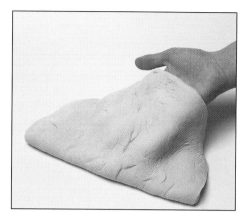

5 ▲ Roll each ball into a 25cm/10in circle. Flip the circles over and on to your palm. Set each circle on the work surface and rotate, stretching the dough as you turn, until it is about 30cm/12in in diameter.

6 ▲ Brush two pizza pans with oil. Place the dough circles in the pans and neaten the edges. Brush with oil.

7 ▲ Cover with the toppings and bake until golden, 10–12 minutes.

Cheese Bread

MAKES 1 LOAF

15ml/1 tbsp active dried yeast
250ml/8fl oz/1 cup lukewarm milk
25g/1oz/2 tbsp butter
425g/15oz/3²/₃ cups strong white bread flour
10ml/2 tsp salt
90g/3¹/₂oz mature Cheddar cheese, grated

1 Combine the yeast and milk. Stir and leave for 15 minutes to dissolve.

2 Melt the butter, leave to cool, and add to the yeast mixture.

3 Mix the flour and salt together in a large bowl. Make a well in the centre and pour in the yeast mixture.

4 With a wooden spoon, stir from the centre, incorporating flour with each turn, to obtain a rough dough. If the dough seems too dry, add 30–45ml/2–3 tbsp water.

5 Transfer to a floured surface and knead until smooth and elastic. Return to the bowl, cover and leave to rise in a warm place until doubled in volume, 2–3 hours.

6 ▲ Grease a 23 × 13cm/9 × 5in loaf tin (pan). Knock back (punch down) the dough with your fist. Knead in the cheese, distributing it as evenly as possible.

7 ▼ Twist the dough, form into a loaf shape and place in the tin, tucking the ends under. Leave in a warm place until the dough rises above the rim of the tin.

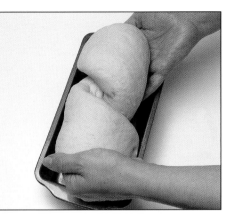

8 ▲ Preheat the oven to 200°C/ 400°F/Gas 6. Bake for 15 minutes, then lower to 190°C/375°F/Gas 5 and bake until the bottom sounds hollow when tapped, about 30 minutes more.

Italian Flat Bread with Sage

MAKES 1 LOAF

10ml/2 tsp active dried yeast
250ml/8fl oz/1 cup lukewarm water
350g/12oz/3 cups strong white bread flour
10ml/2 tsp salt
75ml/5 tbsp extra virgin olive oil
12 fresh sage leaves, chopped

1 Combine the yeast and water, stir and leave for 15 minutes until the yeast has completely dissolved.

2 Mix the flour and salt in a large bowl, and make a well in the centre.

3 Stir in the yeast mixture and 60ml/ 4 tbsp of the oil. Stir from the centre, incorporating flour with each turn, to obtain a rough dough.

4 ▲ Transfer the dough to a lightly floured surface and knead until it is smooth and elastic. Shape into a ball and place in a lightly oiled bowl. Cover and leave to rise in a warm place until doubled in volume, for about 2 hours.

5 Preheat the oven to 200°C/400°F/ Gas 6 and place a baking sheet in the centre of the oven.

6 Knock back (punch down) the dough. Knead in the sage leaves, then roll into a 30cm/12in round. Leave to rise slightly.

7 ▼ Dimple the surface all over with your finger. Drizzle the remaining oil on top. Slide a floured board under the bread, carry to the oven, and slide off on the hot baking sheet. Bake for about 35 minutes, or until golden brown. Cool on a rack.

Courgette Yeast Bread

MAKES 1 LOAF

450g/1lb courgettes (zucchini), grated
30ml/2 tbsp salt
10ml/2 tsp active dried yeast
300ml/½ pint/1¼ cups lukewarm water
400g/14oz/3½ cups strong white bread flour
olive oil, for brushing

1 ▼ In a colander, alternate the layers of grated courgettes and salt. Leave for 30 minutes, then squeeze out the moisture with your hands.

2 Combine yeast with 50ml/2fl oz/¼ cup warm water. Leave for 15 minutes.

3 ▲ Place the courgettes, yeast and flour in a bowl. Stir together and add just enough of the remaining water to obtain a rough dough.

4 Transfer to a floured surface and knead until smooth and elastic. Return the dough to the bowl, cover with a plastic bag, and leave to rise in a warm place until doubled in volume, for about 1½ hours.

5 Knock back (punch down) the risen dough with your fist and knead into a tapered cylinder. Place on a greased baking sheet, cover and leave to rise in a warm place until doubled in volume.

6 ▼ Preheat the oven to 220°C/ 425°F/Gas 7. Brush the bread with olive oil and bake for 40–45 minutes, or until the loaf is a golden colour.

Italian Flat Bread with Sage (top), Courgette Yeast Bread

Olive Bread

MAKES 2 LOAVES

20ml/4 tsp active dried yeast
475ml/16fl oz/2 cups warm water
400g/14oz/3½ cups strong white bread flour
175g/6oz/1½ cups strong wholemeal (whole-wheat) bread flour
65g/2½oz/generous ½ cup cornmeal
10ml/2 tsp salt
30ml/2 tbsp olive oil
115g/4oz/1 cup mixed pitted green and black olives, cut in half
cornmeal, for sprinkling

1 Combine the yeast and water, stir and leave for 5 minutes to dissolve.

2 Stir in 225g/8oz/2 cups of the white flour, cover and leave in a warm place for 1 hour.

3 In a large mixing bowl, combine the remaining white flour, the wholemeal flour, cornmeal and salt. Make a well in the centre; pour in the olive oil and yeast mixture.

4 ▼ With a wooden spoon, stir from the centre, incorporating flour with each turn. When the dough becomes stiff, stir with your hands until a rough dough is obtained.

5 Transfer to a floured surface and knead until smooth and elastic. Return to the bowl, cover and leave to rise in a warm place until doubled in volume, about 1½ hours.

6 ▲ Knock back (punch down) the dough. Add the olives and knead.

7 Cut the dough in half and shape each half into a round. Sprinkle a baking sheet with cornmeal. Place the rounds on the sheet, seam-side down. Cover and leave to rise until nearly doubled in volume.

8 Place a baking tin (pan) in the bottom of the oven and half fill it with hot water. Preheat the oven to 220°C/425°F/Gas 7.

9 ▲ With a sharp knife, score the tops of the loaves. Bake for 20 minutes. Lower the heat to 190°C/375°F/Gas 5 and bake for 25–30 minutes more, or until the bottoms sound hollow when tapped. Cool on a wire rack.

Pumpkin Spice Bread

MAKES 1 LOAF

30ml/2 tbsp active dried yeast
250ml/8fl oz/1 cup lukewarm water
10ml/2 tsp ground cinnamon
5ml/1 tsp ground ginger
5ml/1 tsp ground allspice
1.5ml/^{1}/$_4$ tsp ground cloves
5ml/1 tsp salt
75g/3oz/6 tbsp dried skimmed milk
175g/6oz cooked or canned pumpkin
350g/12oz/1^3/$_4$ cups sugar
115g/4oz/^{1}/$_2$ cup butter, melted
600g/1lb 6oz/5^1/$_2$ cups strong white bread flour
50g/2oz/^{1}/$_3$ cup pecan nuts, finely chopped

1 Using an electric mixer, combine the yeast and water, stir and leave for 15 minutes to dissolve. In another bowl, mix the spices together.

2 To the yeast, add the salt, milk, pumpkin, 115g/4oz/generous ^{1}/$_2$ cup of the sugar, 45ml/3 tbsp of the melted butter, 10ml/2 tsp of the spice mixture and 225g/8oz/2 cups of the flour.

3 ▲ With the dough hook, mix on low speed until blended. Gradually add the remaining flour and mix on medium speed until a rough dough is formed. Alternatively, mix by hand.

4 Transfer to a floured surface and knead until smooth. Place in a bowl, cover and leave to rise in a warm place until doubled, 1–1^1/$_2$ hours.

5 ▼ Knock back (punch down) and knead briefly. Divide the dough into thirds. Roll each third into an 45cm/ 18in rope. Cut each rope into 18 equal pieces, then roll into balls.

6 Grease a 25cm/10in tube tin. Stir the remaining sugar into the remaining spice mixture. Roll the balls in the remaining melted butter, then in the sugar and spice mixture.

7 ▲ Place 18 balls in the tin and sprinkle over half the nuts. Add the remaining balls, then sprinkle over the remaining nuts. Cover and leave to rise in a warm place until almost doubled, about 45 minutes.

8 Preheat the oven to 180°C/350°F/ Gas 4. Bake for 55 minutes. Cool in the tin for 20 minutes, then turn out on a rack. Serve warm.

Walnut Bread

MAKES 1 LOAF

425g/15oz/3²/₃ cups strong wholemeal (whole-wheat) bread flour

150g/5oz/1¹/₄ cups strong white bread flour

12.5ml/2¹/₂ tsp salt

550ml/18fl oz/2¹/₂ cups lukewarm water

15ml/1 tbsp honey

15ml/1 tbsp active dried yeast

150g/5oz/1 cup walnut pieces, plus extra for decorating

1 beaten egg, for glazing

1 Combine the flours and salt in a large bowl. Make a well in the centre and add 250ml/8fl oz/1 cup of the water, the honey and the yeast.

2 Set aside until the yeast dissolves and the mixture is frothy.

3 Add the remaining water. With a wooden spoon, stir from the centre, incorporating flour with each turn, to obtain a smooth dough. Add more flour if the dough is too sticky and use your hands if the dough becomes too stiff to stir.

4 Transfer to a floured board and knead, adding flour if necessary, until the dough is smooth and elastic. Place in a greased bowl and roll the dough around in the bowl to coat thoroughly on all sides.

5 ▲ Cover with a plastic bag and leave in a warm place until doubled in volume, about 1¹/₂ hours.

6 ▲ Knock back (punch down) the dough and knead in the walnuts evenly.

7 Grease a baking sheet. Shape into a round loaf and place on the baking sheet. Press in walnut pieces to decorate the top. Cover and leave to rise in a warm place until doubled, 25–30 minutes.

8 Preheat the oven to 220°C/425°F/ Gas 7.

9 ▲ With a sharp knife, score the top. Brush with the glaze. Bake for 15 minutes. Lower the heat to 190°C/ 375°F/Gas 5 and bake until the bottom sounds hollow when tapped, about 40 minutes. Cool on a rack.

Pecan Rye Bread

MAKES 2 LOAVES

25ml/1¹/₂ tbsp active dried yeast
700ml/24fl oz/2³/₄ cups lukewarm water
670g/1¹/₂lb/6 cups strong white bread flour
505g/1lb 2oz/4¹/₂ cups rye flour
30ml/2 tbsp salt
15ml/1 tbsp honey
10ml/2 tsp caraway seeds, (optional)
115g/4oz/¹/₂ cup butter, at room temperature
225g/8oz/1¹/₃ cups pecan nuts, chopped

1 Combine the yeast and 120ml/ 4fl oz/¹/₂ cup of the water. Stir and leave for 15 minutes to dissolve.

2 In the bowl of an electric mixer, combine the flours, salt, honey, caraway seeds, if using, and butter. With the dough hook, mix on low speed until well blended.

3 Add the yeast mixture and the remaining water and mix on medium speed until the dough forms a ball.

4 ▲ Transfer to a floured surface and knead in the pecan nuts.

5 Return the dough to a bowl, cover with a plastic bag and leave in a warm place until doubled, about 2 hours.

6 Grease two 21 × 12cm/8¹/₂ × 4¹/₂in bread tins (pans).

7 ▲ Knock back (punch down) the risen dough.

8 Divide the dough in half and form into loaves. Place in the tins, seam-side down. Dust the tops with flour. Cover with plastic bags and leave to rise in a warm place until doubled in volume, about 1 hour.

9 Preheat the oven to 190°C/375°F/ Gas 5.

10 ▼ Bake until the bottoms sound hollow when tapped, 45–50 minutes. Cool on racks.

Sticky Buns

MAKES 18

170ml/5¹/₂fl oz/scant ³/₄ cup milk
15ml/1 tbsp active dried yeast
30ml/2 tbsp caster (superfine) sugar
425–450g/15oz–1lb/3¹/₂–4 cups strong white bread flour
5ml/1 tsp salt
115g/4oz/¹/₂ cup cold butter, cut into pieces
2 eggs, lightly beaten
grated rind of 1 lemon
FOR THE TOPPING AND FILLING
275g/10oz/1¹/₄ cups soft dark brown sugar
65g/2¹/₂oz/5 tbsp butter
120ml/4fl oz/¹/₂ cup water
75g/3oz/¹/₂ cup pecan nuts or walnuts, chopped
45ml/3 tbsp caster (superfine) sugar
10ml/2 tsp ground cinnamon
165g/5¹/₂oz/generous 1 cup raisins

1 Heat the milk to lukewarm. Add the yeast and sugar, and leave until frothy, about 15 minutes.

2 Combine the flour and salt in a large mixing bowl. Add the butter and rub in with your fingertips until the mixture resembles coarse breadcrumbs.

3 ▲ Make a well in the centre and add the yeast mixture, eggs and lemon rind. With a wooden spoon, stir from the centre, incorporating flour with each turn. When it becomes too stiff, stir by hand to obtain a rough dough.

4 Transfer to a floured surface and knead until smooth and elastic. Return to the bowl, cover with a plastic bag and leave to rise in a warm place until doubled in volume, about 2 hours.

5 Meanwhile, for the topping, make the syrup. Combine the brown sugar, butter and water in a heavy pan. Bring to the boil and boil gently until thick and syrupy, about 10 minutes.

6 ▲ Place 15ml/1 tbsp of the syrup in the bottom of each of 18 4cm/1¹/₂in muffin cups. Sprinkle in a thin layer of chopped nuts, reserving the rest for the filling.

7 Knock back (punch down) the dough. Roll out to a 45 × 30cm/ 18 × 12in rectangle.

8 ▲ For the filling, combine the caster sugar, cinnamon, raisins and reserved nuts. Sprinkle over the dough in an even layer.

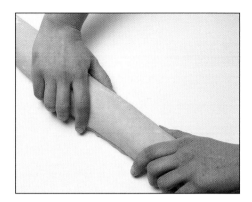

9 ▲ Roll up tightly, from the long side, to form a cylinder.

10 ▲ Cut the cylinder into 2.5cm/ 1in rounds. Place each in a prepared muffin cup, cut-side up. Leave to rise in a warm place until increased by half, about 30 minutes.

11 Preheat the oven to 180°C/350°F/ Gas 4. Place foil under the tins (pans) to catch any syrup that bubbles over. Bake until golden, about 25 minutes.

12 Remove from the oven and invert the tins on to a baking sheet. Leave for 3–5 minutes, then remove the buns from the tins. Transfer to a rack to cool. Serve sticky-side up.

~ COOK'S TIP ~

To save time and energy, make double the recipe and freeze half for another occasion.

Raisin Bread

MAKES 2 LOAVES

15ml/1 tbsp active dried yeast
475ml/16fl oz/2 cups lukewarm milk
150g/5oz/1 cup raisins
65g/2¹/₂oz/generous ¹/₄ cup currants
15ml/1 tbsp sherry or brandy
2.5ml/¹/₂ tsp freshly grated nutmeg
grated rind of 1 large orange
65g/2¹/₂oz/5 tbsp sugar
15ml/1 tbsp salt
115g/4oz/¹/₂ cup butter, melted
700–850g/1¹/₂lb–1lb 14oz/6–7¹/₂ cups strong white bread flour
1 egg beaten with 15ml/1 tbsp cream, for glazing

1 Stir together the yeast and 125ml/ 4fl oz/¹/₂ cup of the milk and leave to stand for 15 minutes to dissolve.

2 ▲ Mix the raisins, currants, sherry or brandy, nutmeg and orange rind together and set aside.

3 In another bowl, mix the remaining milk, sugar, salt and half the butter. Add the yeast mixture. With a wooden spoon, stir in half the flour, 150g/5oz/1¹/₄ cups at a time, until blended. Add the remaining flour as needed for a stiff dough.

4 Transfer to a floured surface and knead until smooth and elastic. Place in a greased bowl, cover and leave to rise in a warm place until doubled in volume, about 2¹/₂ hours.

5 Knock back (punch down) the dough, return to the bowl, cover and leave in a warm place for 30 minutes.

6 Grease two 21 × 12cm/8¹/₂ × 4¹/₂in bread tins (pans). Divide the dough in half and roll each half into a 50 × 18cm/20 × 7in rectangle.

7 ▲ Brush the rectangles with the remaining melted butter. Sprinkle over the raisin mixture, then roll up tightly, tucking in the ends slightly as you roll. Place in the prepared tins, cover, and leave to rise until almost doubled in volume.

8 ▲ Preheat the oven to 200°C/ 400°F/Gas 6. Brush the loaves with the glaze. Bake for 20 minutes. Lower to 180°C/350°F/Gas 4 and bake until golden, 25–30 minutes. Cool on racks.

Prune Bread

MAKES 1 LOAF

225g/8oz/1 cup dried prunes
15ml/1 tbsp active dried yeast
75g/3oz/^{2}/$_3$ cup strong wholemeal (whole-wheat) bread flour
375–425g/13–15oz/3^1/$_4$–3^2/$_3$ cups strong white bread flour
2.5ml/^{1}/$_2$ tsp bicarbonate of soda (baking soda)
5ml/1 tsp salt
5ml/1 tsp pepper
25g/1oz/2 tbsp butter, at room temperature
175ml/6fl oz/^{3}/$_4$ cup buttermilk
50g/2oz/^{1}/$_3$ cup walnuts, chopped
milk, for glazing

1 Simmer the prunes in water to cover until soft, or soak overnight. Drain, reserving 50ml/2fl oz/^{1}/$_4$ cup of the soaking liquid. Pit and chop the prunes.

2 Combine the yeast and the reserved prune liquid. Leave for 15 minutes.

3 In a large bowl, stir together the flours, bicarbonate of soda, salt and pepper. Make a well in the centre.

4 ▲ Add the chopped prunes, butter, and buttermilk. Pour in the yeast mixture. With a wooden spoon, stir from the centre, incorporating more flour with each turn, to obtain a rough dough.

5 Transfer to a floured surface and knead until smooth and elastic. Return to the bowl, cover with a plastic bag and leave to rise in a warm place until doubled in volume, about 1^1/$_2$ hours.

6 Grease a baking sheet.

7 ▲ Punch down the dough with your fist, then knead in the walnuts.

8 Shape the dough into a long, cylindrical loaf. Place on the baking sheet, cover loosely, and leave to rise in a warm place for 45 minutes.

9 Preheat the oven to 220°C/425°F/ Gas 7.

10 ▼ With a sharp knife, score the top deeply. Brush with milk and bake for 15 minutes. Lower to 190°C/375°F/ Gas 5 and bake until the bottom sounds hollow when tapped, 35 minutes. Cool.

Braided Prune Bread

MAKES 1 LOAF

15ml/1 tbsp active dried yeast
50ml/2fl oz/¼ cup lukewarm water
50ml/2fl oz/¼ cup lukewarm milk
50g/2oz/¼ cup caster (superfine) sugar
2.5ml/½ tsp salt
1 egg
50g/2oz/¼ cup butter, at room temperature
425–505g/15oz–1lb 2oz/3²/₃–4¹/₂ cups strong white bread flour
1 egg beaten with 10ml/2 tsp water, for glazing

FOR THE FILLING

200g/7oz/scant 1 cup cooked prunes, pitted
10ml/2 tsp grated lemon rind
5ml/1 tsp grated orange rind
1.5ml/¼ tsp freshly grated nutmeg
40g/1½oz/3 tbsp butter, melted
50g/2oz/¼ cup very finely chopped walnuts
25g/1oz/2 tbsp caster sugar

1 In a large bowl, combine the yeast and water, stir and leave for 15 minutes to dissolve.

2 Stir in the milk, sugar, salt, egg and butter. Gradually stir in 350g/12oz/3 cups of the flour to obtain a soft dough.

3 Transfer to a floured surface and knead in just enough flour to obtain a dough that is smooth and elastic. Put into a clean bowl, cover and leave to rise in a warm place until doubled in volume, about 1¹/₂ hours.

~ VARIATION ~

For Plaited Apricot Bread, replace the prunes with the same amount of dried apricots. It is not necessary to cook them, but, to soften, soak them in hot tea and discard the liquid before using.

4 ▲ Meanwhile, for the filling, combine the prunes, lemon and orange rinds, nutmeg, butter, walnuts and sugar, and stir together to blend. Set aside.

5 Grease a large baking sheet. Knock back (punch down) the dough and transfer to a lightly floured surface. Knead briefly, then roll out into a 38 × 25cm/15 × 10in rectangle. Carefully transfer to the baking sheet.

6 ▲ Spread the filling in the centre.

7 ▲ With a sharp knife, cut ten strips at an angle on either side of the filling, cutting just to the filling.

8 ▲ For a braided pattern, fold up one end neatly, then fold over the strips from alternating sides until all the strips are folded over. Tuck excess dough underneath at the ends.

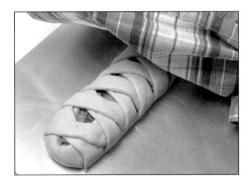

9 ▲ Cover loosely with a dish towel and leave to rise in a warm place until almost doubled in volume.

10 ▲ Preheat the oven to 190°C/375°F/Gas 5. Brush with the glaze. Bake until browned, about 30 minutes. Transfer to a rack to cool.

Kugelhopf

MAKES 1 LOAF

115g/4oz/²/³ cup raisins

15ml/1 tbsp Kirsch or brandy

15ml/1 tbsp active dried yeast

120ml/4fl oz/¹/² cup lukewarm water

115g/4oz/¹/² cup unsalted (sweet) butter, at room temperature

90g/3¹/²oz/¹/² cup sugar

3 eggs, at room temperature

grated rind of 1 lemon

5ml/1 tsp salt

2.5ml/¹/² tsp vanilla extract

425g/15oz/3²/³ cups strong white bread flour

120ml/4fl oz/¹/² cup milk

25g/1oz/¹/⁴ cup flaked (sliced) almonds

90g/3¹/²oz/scant 1 cup whole blanched almonds, chopped

icing (confectioners') sugar, for dusting

1 ▼ In a bowl, combine the raisins and Kirsch or brandy. Set aside.

2 Combine the yeast and water, stir and leave for 15 minutes to dissolve.

3 With an electric mixer, cream the butter and sugar until thick and fluffy. Beat in the eggs, one at a time. Add the lemon rind, salt and vanilla. Stir in the yeast mixture.

4 ▲ Add the flour, alternating with the milk, until the mixture is well blended. Cover and leave to rise in a warm place until doubled in volume, about 2 hours.

5 ▲ Grease a 4¹/² pint Kugelhopf mould, then sprinkle the flaked almonds evenly over the bottom.

6 Work the raisins and whole almonds into the dough, then spoon into the mould. Cover with a plastic bag, and leave to rise in a warm place until the dough almost reaches the top of the mould, about 1 hour.

7 Preheat the oven to 180°C/350°F/ Gas 4.

8 Bake until golden brown, about 45 minutes. If the top browns too quickly, protect with a sheet of foil. Leave to cool in the mould for 15 minutes, then turn out on to a rack. Dust the top lightly with icing sugar before serving.

Panettone

MAKES 1 LOAF

150ml/¼ pint/⅔ cup lukewarm milk
15ml/1 tbsp active dried yeast
350–400g/12–14oz/3–3½ cups strong white bread flour
65g/2½oz/5 tbsp sugar
10ml/2 tsp salt
2 eggs
5 egg yolks
175g/6oz/¾ cup unsalted (sweet) butter, at room temperature
130g/4½oz/scant 1 cup raisins
grated rind of 1 lemon
75g/3oz/½ cup mixed peel

1 Combine the milk and yeast in a large warmed bowl and leave for 10 minutes to dissolve.

2 Stir in 115g/4oz/1 cup of the flour, cover loosely and leave in a warm place for 30 minutes.

3 Sift over the remaining flour and stir into the dough mixture. Make a well in the centre and add the sugar, salt, eggs and egg yolks.

4 ▲ Stir with a wooden spoon until stiff, then stir with your hands to obtain a very elastic and sticky dough. Add a little more flour if necessary, but keep the dough as soft as possible.

5 ▲ To incorporate the butter, smear it over the dough, then work it in with your hands. When the butter is evenly distributed, cover and leave to rise in a warm place until doubled in volume, 3–4 hours.

6 Grease a 2 litre/3½ pint/9 cup charlotte tin (pan) or a 1kg/2¼lb coffee tin and line the bottom with baking parchment. Grease the paper.

7 Knock back (punch down) the dough. Knead in the raisins, lemon rind and mixed peel.

8 ▲ Put the dough in the tin. Cover and leave to rise in a warm place until it is well above the top of the tin, about 2 hours.

9 Preheat the oven to 200°C/400°F/ Gas 6. Bake for 15 minutes, cover the top with foil and lower the heat to 180°C/350°F/Gas 4. Bake for 30 minutes more. Cool in the tin for 5 minutes, then transfer to a rack.

Danish Wreath

10g/¹/₄oz active dried yeast

175ml/6fl oz/³/₄ cup lukewarm milk

50g/2oz/¹/₄ cup caster (superfine) sugar

450g/1lb/4 cups strong white bread flour

2.5ml/¹/₂ tsp salt

2.5ml/¹/₂ tsp vanilla extract

1 egg, beaten

225g/8oz/1 cup blocks unsalted (sweet) butter

1 egg yolk beaten with 10ml/2 tsp water, for glazing

115g/4oz/1 cup icing (confectioners') sugar

15–30ml/1–2 tbsp water

chopped pecan nuts or walnuts, for sprinkling

FOR THE FILLING

200g/7oz/scant 1 cup soft dark brown sugar

5ml/1 tsp ground cinnamon

50g/2oz/¹/₃ cup pecan nuts or walnuts, toasted and chopped

1 Combine the yeast, milk and 2.5ml/¹/₂ tsp of the sugar. Stir and leave for 15 minutes to dissolve.

2 Combine the flour, sugar and salt. Make a well in the centre and add the yeast mixture, vanilla and egg. Stir until a rough dough is formed.

3 Transfer to a floured surface and knead until smooth and elastic. Wrap and chill for 15 minutes.

~ VARIATION ~

For a different filling, substitute 3 tart apples, peeled and grated, the grated rind of 1 lemon, 15ml/1 tbsp lemon juice, 2.5ml/¹/₂ tsp ground cinnamon, 45ml/3 tbsp sugar, 35g/1¹/₄oz/1¹/₄ tbsp currants, and 25g/1oz/2 tbsp chopped walnuts. Combine well and use as described.

4 ▲ Meanwhile, place the butter between two sheets of baking parchment. With a rolling pin, flatten to form two 15 × 10cm/6 × 4in rectangles. Set aside.

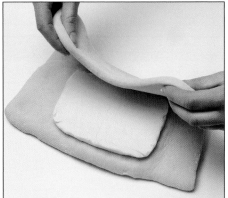

5 ▲ Roll out the dough to a 30 × 20cm/12 × 8in rectangle. Place one butter rectangle in the centre. Fold the bottom third of dough over the butter and seal the edge. Place the other butter rectangle on top and cover with the top third of the dough.

6 Turn the dough so the shorter side faces you. Roll into a 30 × 20cm/12 × 8in rectangle. Fold into thirds, and indent one edge with your finger to indicate the first turn. Wrap in clear film (plastic wrap) and chill for 30 minutes.

7 Repeat two more times; rolling, folding, marking and chilling between each turn. After the third fold chill for 1–2 hours, or longer.

8 Grease a large baking sheet. In a bowl, stir together all the filling ingredients until blended.

9 ▲ Roll out the dough to a 62 × 15cm/ 25 × 6in strip. Spread over the filling, leaving a 1cm/¹/₂in border.

10 Roll up the dough lengthways into a cylinder. Place on the baking sheet and form into a circle, pinching the edges together to seal. Cover with an inverted bowl and leave in a warm place to rise for 45 minutes.

11 ▲ Preheat the oven to 200°C/ 400°F/Gas 6. Slash the top every 5cm/2in, cutting about 1cm/¹/₂in deep. Brush with the egg glaze. Bake until golden, 35–40 minutes. Cool on a rack. To serve, mix the icing sugar and water, then drizzle over the wreath. Sprinkle with the pecan nuts or walnuts.

PIES & TARTS

HERE IS EVERY SORT OF FILLING –
FROM ORCHARD FRUITS TO AUTUMN
NUTS, TANGY CITRUS TO LUSCIOUS
CHOCOLATE – FOR THE MOST
MEMORABLE PIES AND TARTS. SOME
ARE PLAIN AND SOME ARE FANCY,
BUT ALL ARE DELICIOUS.

Plum Pie

SERVES 8

900g/2lb red or purple plums

grated rind of 1 lemon

15ml/1 tbsp lemon juice

115–175g/4–6oz/³⁄₄–scant 1 cup caster
(superfine) sugar

45ml/3 tbsp quick-cooking tapioca

pinch of salt

2.5ml/¹⁄₂ tsp ground cinnamon

1.5ml/¹⁄₄ tsp freshly grated nutmeg

FOR THE PASTRY

275g/10oz/2¹⁄₂ cups plain (all-purpose) flour

5ml/1 tsp salt

75g/3oz/6 tbsp cold butter, cut in pieces

50g/2oz/¹⁄₄ cup cold white vegetable fat
(shortening), cut in pieces

50–120ml/2–4fl oz/¹⁄₄–¹⁄₂ cup iced water

milk, for glazing

1 ▼ For the pastry, sift the flour and salt into a bowl. Add the butter and fat and cut in with a pastry blender until the mixture resembles coarse breadcrumbs.

2 Stir in just enough water to bind the pastry. Gather into two balls, one slightly larger than the other. Wrap and chill for 20 minutes.

3 Preheat a baking sheet in the centre of a 220°C/425°F/Gas 7 oven.

4 On a lightly floured surface, roll out the larger pastry ball to about 3mm/¹⁄₈in thick. Transfer to a 23cm/9in pie dish and trim the edge.

5 ▲ Halve the plums, discard the stones (pits), and cut into large pieces. Mix all the filling ingredients together (if the plums are tart, use extra sugar). Transfer to the pastry case (pie shell).

6 ▲ Roll out the remaining pastry and place on a baking tray lined with baking parchment. With a cutter, stamp out four hearts. Transfer the pastry lid to the pie using the paper.

7 Trim to leave a 2cm/³⁄₄in overhang. Fold the top edge under the bottom and pinch to seal. Arrange the hearts on top. Brush with the milk. Bake for 15 minutes. Reduce the heat to 180°C/350°F/Gas 4 and bake for 30–35 minutes more. If the crust browns too quickly, protect with a sheet of foil.

Lattice Berry Pie

SERVES 8

450g/1lb/4 cups berries, such as bilberries, blueberries, blackcurrants etc

115g/4oz/generous ¹/₂ cup caster (superfine) sugar

45ml/3 tbsp cornflour (cornstarch)

30ml/2 tbsp lemon juice

25g/1oz/2 tbsp butter, diced

FOR THE PASTRY

275g/10oz/2¹/₂ cups plain (all-purpose) flour

4ml/³/₄ tsp salt

115g/4oz/¹/₂ cup cold butter, cut in pieces

40g/1¹/₂oz/3 tbsp cold white vegetable fat (shortening), cut in pieces

75–90ml/5–6 tbsp iced water

1 egg beaten with 15ml/1 tbsp water, for glazing

1 For the pastry, sift the flour and salt into a bowl. Add the butter and fat, and cut in with a pastry blender until the mixture resembles coarse breadcrumbs. With a fork, stir in just enough water to bind the pastry. Form into two balls, wrap in baking parchment, and chill for 20 minutes.

2 On a lightly floured surface, roll out one ball about 3mm/¹/₈in thick. Transfer to a 23cm/9in pie dish and trim to leave a 1cm/¹/₂in overhang. Brush the base with egg glaze.

3 ▲ Mix all the filling ingredients together, except the butter (reserve a few berries for decoration). Spoon into the pastry case and dot with the butter. Brush the egg glaze around the rim of the pastry case (pie shell).

4 Preheat a baking sheet in the centre of a 220°C/425°F/Gas 7 oven.

5 ▼ Roll out the remaining pastry on a baking tray lined with baking parchment. With a serrated pastry wheel, cut out 24 thin pastry strips. Roll out the scraps and cut out leaf shapes. Mark veins in the leaves with the point of a knife.

6 ▲ Weave the strips in a close lattice, then transfer to the pie using the paper. Press the edges to seal and trim. Arrange the pastry leaves around the rim. Brush with egg glaze.

7 Bake for 10 minutes. Reduce the heat to 180°C/350°F/Gas 4 and bake until the pastry is golden, 40–45 minutes more. Decorate with berries.

Raspberry Tart

SERVES 8

4 egg yolks	
65g/2½oz/5 tbsp caster (superfine) sugar	
45ml/3 tbsp plain (all-purpose) flour	
300ml/½ pint/1¼ cups milk	
pinch of salt	
2.5ml/½ tsp vanilla extract	
450g/1lb/2⅔ cups fresh raspberries	
75ml/5 tbsp red currant jelly	
15ml/1 tbsp fresh orange juice	

FOR THE PASTRY

190g/6½oz/1⅔ cups plain (all-purpose) flour	
2.5ml/½ tsp baking powder	
1.5ml/¼ tsp salt	
15ml/1 tbsp sugar	
grated rind of ½ orange	
75g/3oz/6 tbsp cold butter, cut in pieces	
1 egg yolk	
45–60ml/3–4 tbsp whipping cream	

1 For the pastry, sift the flour, baking powder and salt into a bowl. Stir in the sugar and orange rind. Add the butter and cut in with a pastry blender until the mixture resembles coarse breadcrumbs. Stir in the egg yolk and just enough cream to bind the dough. Gather into a ball, wrap in baking parchment and chill.

2 For the custard filling, beat the egg yolks and sugar until thick and lemon-coloured. Gradually stir in the flour.

3 In a pan, bring the milk and salt just to the boil, then remove from the heat. Whisk into the egg yolk mixture, return to the pan and continue whisking over medium high heat until just bubbling. Cook for 3 minutes to thicken. Transfer immediately to a bowl. Add the vanilla and stir to blend.

4 ▲ Cover with baking parchment to prevent a skin from forming.

5 ▲ Preheat the oven to 200°C/400°F/Gas 6. On a floured surface, roll out the pastry 3mm/⅛in thick, transfer to a 25cm/10in pie dish and trim. Prick the base with a fork and line with crumpled baking parchment. Fill with baking beans and bake for 15 minutes. Remove the paper and beans. Continue baking until golden, 6–8 minutes more. Leave to cool.

6 ▲ Spread an even layer of the pastry cream filling in the pastry case (pie shell) and arrange the raspberries on top. Melt the jelly and orange juice in a pan and brush on top to glaze.

Rhubarb and Cherry Pie

SERVES 8

450g/1lb rhubarb, cut into
2.5cm/1in pieces

450g/1lb canned pitted tart red or black
cherries, drained

275g/10oz/1½ cups caster (superfine) sugar

25g/1oz quick-cooking tapioca

FOR THE PASTRY

275g/10oz/2½ cups plain (all-purpose) flour

5ml/1 tsp salt

75g/3oz/6 tbsp cold butter, cut in pieces

50g/2oz/⅓ cup cold white vegetable fat
(shortening), cut in pieces

50–120ml/2–4fl oz/¼–½ cup iced water

milk, for glazing

1 ▲ For the pastry, sift the flour and salt into a bowl. Add the butter and fat to the dry ingredients and cut in with a pastry blender until the mixture resembles coarse breadcrumbs.

2 With a fork, stir in just enough water to bind the pastry. Gather into two balls, one slightly larger than the other. Wrap the pastry in baking parchment and chill for at least 20 minutes.

3 Preheat a baking sheet in the centre of a 200°C/400°F/Gas 6 oven.

4 On a lightly floured surface, roll out the larger pastry ball to a thickness of about 3mm/⅛in.

5 ▼ Roll the pastry around the rolling pin and transfer to a 23cm/9in pie dish. Trim the edge to leave a 1cm/½in overhang.

6 Chill the pastry case (pie shell) while making the filling.

7 In a mixing bowl, combine the rhubarb, cherries, sugar and tapioca, and spoon into the pie shell.

8 ▲ Roll out the remaining pastry and cut out leaf shapes.

9 Transfer the pastry lid to the pie and trim to leave a 2cm/¾in overhang. Fold the top edge under the bottom, and flute. Roll small balls from the scraps. Mark veins in the pastry leaves and place on top with the balls.

10 Glaze the top and bake until golden, 40–50 minutes.

Peach Leaf Pie

SERVES 8

1.2kg/2^1/$_2$lb ripe peaches
juice of 1 lemon
90g/3^1/$_2$oz/^{1}/$_2$ cup caster (superfine) sugar
45ml/3 tbsp cornflour (cornstarch)
1.5ml/^{1}/$_4$ tsp grated nutmeg
2.5ml/^{1}/$_2$ tsp ground cinnamon
25g/1oz/2 tbsp butter, diced
FOR THE CRUST
275g/10oz/2^1/$_2$ cups plain (all-purpose) flour
4ml/^{3}/$_4$ tsp salt
115g/4oz/^{1}/$_2$ cup cold butter, cut into pieces
60g/2^1/$_4$oz/generous ^{1}/$_3$ cup cold white vegetable fat (shortening), cut into pieces
60–75ml/5–6 tbsp iced water
1 egg beaten with 15ml/1 tbsp water, for glazing

1 For the pastry, sift the flour and salt into a bowl. Add the butter and fat and rub in with your fingertips until the mixture resembles coarse breadcrumbs.

2 ▲ With a fork, stir in just enough water to bind the dough. Gather into two balls, one slightly larger than the other. Wrap in clear film (plastic wrap) and chill for 20 minutes.

3 Place a baking sheet in the oven and preheat to 220°C/425°F/Gas 7.

4 ▲ Drop a few peaches at a time into boiling water for 20 seconds, then transfer to a bowl of cold water. When cool, peel off the skins.

5 Slice the peaches and combine with the lemon juice, sugar, cornflour and spices. Set aside.

6 ▲ On a lightly floured surface, roll out the larger dough ball to about 3mm/^{1}/$_8$in thick. Transfer to a 23cm/9in pie tin (pan) and trim. Chill.

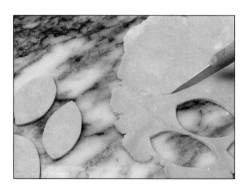

7 ▲ Roll out the remaining dough 5mm/^{1}/$_4$in thick. Cut out leaf shapes 7.5cm/3in long, using a template if needed. Mark veins with a knife. With the scraps, roll a few balls.

8 ▲ Brush the bottom of the pastry case (pie shell) with egg glaze. Add the peaches, piling them higher in the centre. Dot with the butter.

9 ▲ To assemble, start from the outside edge and cover the peaches with a ring of leaves. Place a second ring of leaves above, staggering the positions. Continue with rows of leaves until covered. Place the balls in the centre. Brush with glaze.

10 Bake for 10 minutes. Lower the heat to 180°C/350°F/Gas 4 and bake for 35–40 minutes more.

~ COOK'S TIP ~

Baking the pie on a preheated baking sheet helps to make the bottom crust crisp. The moisture from the filling keeps the bottom crust more humid than the top, but this baking method helps to compensate for the top crust being more exposed to the heat source.

Peach Tart with Almond Cream

4 large ripe peaches

115g/4oz/²/₃ cup blanched almonds

30ml/2 tbsp plain (all-purpose) flour

90g/3¹/₂oz/7 tbsp unsalted (sweet) butter, at room temperature

115g/4oz/¹/₂ cup plus 30ml/2 tbsp caster (superfine) sugar

1 egg

1 egg yolk

2.5ml/¹/₂ tsp vanilla extract, or 10ml/2 tsp rum

FOR THE PASTRY

190g/6¹/₂oz/1²/₃ cups plain (all-purpose) flour

4ml/³/₄ tsp salt

90g/3¹/₂oz/7 tbsp cold unsalted (sweet) butter, cut in pieces

1 egg yolk

40–45ml/2¹/₂–3 tbsp iced water

1 ▲ For the pastry, sift the flour and salt into a bowl.

2 Add the butter and cut in with a pastry blender until the mixture resembles coarse breadcrumbs. Stir in the egg yolk and just enough water to bind the pastry. Gather into a ball, wrap in baking parchment and chill for at least 20 minutes.

3 Preheat a baking sheet in the centre of a 200°C/400°F/Gas 6 oven.

4 ▲ On a floured surface, roll out the pastry to 3mm/¹/₈in thick. Transfer to a 25cm/10in pie dish. Trim the edge, prick the base and chill.

5 ▲ Score the bottoms of the peaches. Drop the peaches, one at a time, into boiling water. Boil for 20 seconds, then dip in cold water. Peel off the skins using a sharp knife.

6 ▲ Grind the almonds finely with the flour in a food processor, blender or grinder. With an electric mixer, cream the butter and 115g/4oz/generous ¹/₂ cup of the sugar until light and fluffy. Gradually beat in the egg and yolk. Stir in the almonds and vanilla or rum. Spread in the pastry case(pie shell).

7 ▲ Halve the peaches and remove the stones (pits). Cut crossways in thin slices and arrange on top of the almond cream like the spokes of a wheel; keep the slices of each peach-half together. Fan out by pressing down gently at a slight angle.

8 ▲ Bake until the pastry begins to brown, 10–15 minutes. Lower the heat to 180°C/350°F/Gas 4 and continue baking until the almond cream sets, about 15 minutes more. Ten minutes before the end of the cooking time, sprinkle with the remaining 30ml/2 tbsp of sugar.

~ VARIATION ~

For a Nectarine and Apricot Tart with Almond Cream, replace the peaches with nectarines, prepared and arranged the same way. Peel and chop three fresh apricots. Fill the spaces between the fanned-out nectarines with 15ml/1 tbsp of chopped apricots. Bake as above.

Apple and Cranberry Lattice Pie

SERVES 8

grated rind of 1 orange

45ml/3 tbsp fresh orange juice

2 large, tart cooking apples

175g/6oz/1½ cups cranberries

65g/2½oz/½ cup raisins

25g/1oz/2 tbsp walnuts, chopped

215g/7½oz/generous 1 cup caster (superfine) sugar

115g/4oz/½ cup soft dark brown sugar

30ml/2 tbsp plain (all-purpose) flour

FOR THE CRUST

275g/10oz/2½ cups plain flour

2.5ml/½ tsp salt

75g/3oz/6 tbsp cold butter, cut into pieces

75g/3oz/½ cup cold white vegetable fat (shortening), cut into pieces

60–120ml/2–4fl oz/¼–½ cup iced water

1 ▼ For the crust, sift the flour and salt into a bowl. Add the butter and fat and rub in with your fingertips until the mixture resembles coarse breadcrumbs. With a fork, stir in just enough water to bind the dough. Gather into two equal balls, wrap in clear film (plastic wrap), and chill for at least 20 minutes.

2 ▲ Put the orange rind and juice into a mixing bowl. Peel and core the apples and grate into the bowl. Stir in the cranberries, raisins, walnuts, all except 15g/½oz/1 tbsp of the caster sugar, the brown sugar and flour.

3 Place a baking sheet in the oven and preheat to 200°C/400°F/Gas 6.

4 On a lightly floured surface, roll out one ball of dough to about 3mm/⅛in thick. Transfer to a 23cm/9in pie plate and trim. Spoon the cranberry and apple mixture into the pastry case (pie shell).

5 ▲ Roll out the remaining dough to a circle about 28cm/11in in diameter. With a serrated pastry wheel, cut the dough into ten strips, 2cm/¾in wide. Place five strips horizontally across the top of the tart at 2.5cm/1in intervals. Weave in five vertical strips and trim. Sprinkle the top with the remaining sugar.

6 Bake the pie for 20 minutes. Reduce the heat to 180°C/350°F/ Gas 4 and bake for about 15 minutes more, until the crust is golden and the filling is bubbling.

Open Apple Pie

SERVES 8

1.3kg/3lb sweet, tart firm eating or cooking apples
50g/2oz/¹/₄ cup caster (superfine) sugar
10ml/2 tsp ground cinnamon
grated rind and juice of 1 lemon
25g/1oz/2 tbsp butter, diced
30–45ml/2–3 tbsp honey
FOR THE CRUST
275g/10oz/2¹/₂ cups plain (all-purpose) flour
2.5ml/¹/₂ tsp salt
115g/4oz/¹/₂ cup cold butter, cut into pieces
60g/2¹/₄oz/generous ¹/₃ cup cold white vegetable fat (shortening), cut into pieces
75–90ml/5–6 tbsp iced water

1 For the crust, sift the flour and salt into a bowl. Add the butter and fat and rub in with your fingertips until the mixture resembles coarse breadcrumbs.

2 ▲ With a fork, stir in just enough water to bind the dough. Gather into a ball, wrap in clear film (plastic wrap), and chill for at least 20 minutes.

3 Place a baking sheet in the centre of the oven and preheat to 200°C/400°F/Gas 6.

4 ▼ Peel, core, and slice the apples. Combine the sugar and cinnamon in a bowl. Add the apples, lemon rind and juice, and stir.

5 On a lightly floured surface, roll out the dough to a circle about 30cm/12in in diameter. Transfer to a 23cm/9in diameter deep pie dish; leave the dough hanging over the edge. Fill with the apple slices.

6 ▲ Fold in the edges and crimp loosely for a decorative border. Dot the apples with diced butter.

7 Bake on the hot sheet until the pastry is golden and the apples are tender, about 45 minutes.

8 Melt the honey in a pan and brush over the apples to glaze. Serve warm or at room temperature.

Apple Pie

SERVES 8

900g/2lb tart cooking apples
30ml/2 tbsp plain (all-purpose) flour
115g/4oz/generous 1/2 cup caster (superfine) sugar
25ml/1 1/2 tbsp fresh lemon juice
2.5ml/1/2 tsp ground cinnamon
2.5ml/1/2 tsp ground allspice
1.5ml/1/4 tsp ground ginger
1.5ml/1/4 tsp freshly grated nutmeg
1.5ml/1/4 tsp salt
50g/2oz/1/4 cup butter, diced
FOR THE PASTRY
275g/10oz/2 1/2 cups plain (all-purpose) flour
5ml/1 tsp salt
75g/3oz/6 tbsp cold butter, cut in pieces
50g/2oz/1/3 cup cold white vegetable fat (shortening), cut in pieces
50–120ml/2–4fl oz/1/4–1/2 cup iced water

1 ▲ For the crust, sift the flour and salt into a bowl.

2 Add the butter and fat and cut in with a pastry blender or rub between your fingertips until the mixture resembles coarse breadcrumbs. With a fork, stir in just enough water to bind the pastry.

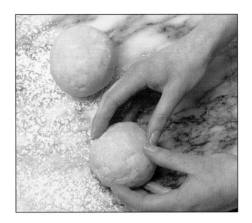

3 ▲ Form two balls, wrap in clear film (plastic wrap). Chill for 20 minutes.

4 ▲ On a lightly floured surface, roll out one ball 3mm/1/8in thick. Transfer to a 23cm/9in pie dish and trim the edge. Preheat a baking sheet in the centre of a 220°C/425°F/Gas 7 oven.

5 ▲ Peel, core and slice the apples into a bowl. Toss with the flour, sugar, lemon juice, spices and salt. Spoon into the pastry case (pie shell), dot with butter.

6 ▲ Roll out the remaining pastry. Place on top of the pie and trim to leave a 2cm/3/4in overhang. Fold the overhang under the pastry base and press to seal. Crimp the edge.

7 ▲ Roll out the scraps and cut out leaf shapes and roll balls. Arrange on top of the pie. Cut steam vents.

8 Bake for 10 minutes. Reduce the heat to 180°C/350°F/Gas 4 and bake until golden, 40–45 minutes more. If the pie browns too quickly, protect with foil.

~ COOK'S TIP ~

Instead of using cooking apples, choose crisp eaters such as Granny Smith, which will not soften too much during cooking.

Pear and Apple Crumble Pie

SERVES 8

3 firm pears

4 cooking apples

175g/6oz/scant 1 cup caster (superfine) sugar

30ml/2 tbsp cornflour (cornstarch)

pinch of salt

grated rind of 1 lemon

30ml/2 tbsp fresh lemon juice

75g/3oz/²⁄₃ cup raisins

75g/3oz/²⁄₃ cup plain (all-purpose) flour

5ml/1 tsp ground cinnamon

75g/3oz/6 tbsp cold butter, cut in pieces

FOR THE PASTRY

150g/5oz/1¹⁄₄ cups plain flour

2.5ml/¹⁄₂ tsp salt

65g/2¹⁄₂oz/scant ¹⁄₂ cup cold white vegetable fat (shortening), cut in pieces

30ml/2 tbsp iced water

1 For the pastry, combine the flour and salt in a bowl. Add the fat and cut in with a pastry blender until the mixture resembles coarse breadcrumbs. Stir in just enough water to bind the pastry. Gather into a ball and transfer to a lightly floured surface. Roll out 3mm/¹⁄₈in thick.

2 ▲ Transfer to a shallow 23cm/9in pie dish and trim to leave a 1cm/¹⁄₂in overhang. Fold the overhang under for double thickness. Flute the edge. Chill.

3 Preheat a baking sheet in the centre of a 230°C/450°F/Gas 8 oven.

4 ▲ Peel and core the pears. Slice them into a bowl. Peel, core and slice the apples. Add to the pears. Stir in one-third of the sugar, the cornflour, salt and lemon rind. Add the lemon juice and raisins, and stir to blend.

5 For the crumble topping, combine the remaining sugar, flour, cinnamon, and butter in a bowl. Blend with your fingertips until the mixture resembles coarse breadcrumbs. Set aside.

6 ▲ Spoon the fruit filling into the pastry case (pie shell). Sprinkle the crumbs lightly and evenly over the top.

7 Bake for 10 minutes, then reduce the heat to 180°C/350°F/Gas 4. Cover the top of the pie loosely with a sheet of foil and continue baking until browned, 35–40 minutes more.

Chocolate Pear Tart

SERVES 8

115g/4oz plain (semisweet) chocolate, grated
3 large firm, ripe pears
1 egg
1 egg yolk
120ml/4fl oz/½ cup single (light) cream
2.5ml/½ tsp vanilla extract
45ml/3 tbsp caster (superfine) sugar
FOR THE PASTRY
150g/5oz/1¼ cups plain (all-purpose) flour
pinch of salt
30ml/2 tbsp sugar
115g/4oz/½ cup cold unsalted (sweet) butter, cut into pieces
1 egg yolk
15ml/1 tbsp fresh lemon juice

1 For the pastry, sift the flour and salt into a bowl. Add the sugar and butter. Cut in with a pastry blender until the mixture resembles coarse breadcrumbs. Stir in the egg yolk and lemon juice until the mixture forms a ball. Wrap in clear film (plastic wrap) and chill for at least 20 minutes.

2 Preheat a baking sheet in the centre of a 200°C/400°F/Gas 6 oven.

3 On a lightly floured surface, roll out the pastry 3mm/⅛in thick. Transfer to a 25cm/10in tart dish and trim.

4 ▲ Sprinkle the base of the pastry case (pie shell) with the grated chocolate.

5 ▲ Peel, halve and core the pears. Cut in thin slices crossways, then fan them out slightly.

6 Transfer the pear halves to the tart with the help of a metal spatula and arrange on top of the chocolate like the spokes of a wheel.

7 ▼ Whisk together the egg and egg yolk, cream and vanilla. Ladle over the pears, then sprinkle with sugar.

8 Bake for 10 minutes. Reduce the heat to 180°C/350°F/Gas 4 and cook until the custard is set and the pears begin to caramelize, about 20 minutes more. Serve warm.

Caramelized Upside-down Pear Pie

SERVES 8

5–6 firm, ripe pears

175g/6oz/scant 1 cup sugar

115g/4oz/¹/₂ cup unsalted (sweet) butter

whipped cream, for serving

FOR THE PASTRY

115g/4oz/1 cup plain (all-purpose) flour

1.5ml/¹/₄ tsp salt

130g/4¹/₂oz/generous ¹/₂ cup cold butter,
   cut into pieces

40g/1¹/₂oz/¹/₄ cup cold white vegetable fat
   (shortening), cut into pieces

60ml/4 tbsp iced water

1 ▲ For the pastry, combine the flour and salt in a bowl. Add the butter and vegetable fat and cut in with a pastry blender until the mixture resembles coarse crumbs. With a fork, stir in enough iced water to bind the dough. Gather into a ball, wrap in clear film (plastic wrap) and chill for at least 20 minutes. Preheat the oven to 200°C/400°F/Gas 6.

~ **VARIATION** ~

For Caramelized Upside-Down Apple Pie, replace the pears with 8–9 firm, tart apples. There may seem to be too many apples, but they shrink slightly as they cook.

2 ▲ Quarter, peel and core the pears. Place in a bowl and toss with a few tablespoons of the sugar.

3 ▲ In a 27cm/10¹/₂in ovenproof frying pan, melt the butter over moderately high heat. Add the remaining sugar. When it starts to colour, arrange the pears evenly around the edge and in the centre.

4 ▲ Continue cooking, uncovered, until caramelized, about 20 minutes.

5 ▲ Leave the fruit to cool. Roll out a circle of dough slightly larger than the diameter of the pan. Place the dough on top of the pears, tucking it around the edges. Transfer the pan to the oven and bake for 15 minutes, then reduce the heat to 180°C/350°F/Gas 4. Bake until golden, about 15 minutes more.

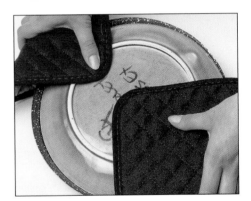

6 ▲ Let the pie cool in the pan for about 3–4 minutes. Run a knife around the edge of the pan to loosen the pie, ensuring that the knife reaches down to the bottom of the pan. Invert a plate on top and, protecting your hands with oven gloves, hold plate and pan firmly, and turn them both over quickly.

7 Lift off the pan. If any pears stick to the pan, remove them gently with a metal spatula and replace them carefully on the pie. Serve warm, with the whipped cream passed round separately.

Lime Tart

SERVES 8

3 large egg yolks

1 × 400g/14oz can sweetened
condensed milk

15ml/1 tbsp grated lime rind

120ml/4fl oz/¹/₂ cup fresh lime juice

green food colouring (optional)

120ml/4fl oz/¹/₂ cup whipping cream

FOR THE BASE

115g/4oz/2 cups digestive biscuits
(graham crackers), crushed

65g/2¹/₂oz/5 tbsp butter or
margarine, melted

1 Preheat the oven to 180°C/350°F/
Gas 4.

2 ▲ For the base, place the crushed
biscuits in a bowl and add the butter
or margarine. Mix to combine.

> ~ VARIATION ~
>
> Use lemons instead of limes,
> with yellow food colouring.

3 Press the mixture evenly over the
base and sides of a 23cm/9in pie dish.
Bake for 8 minutes. Leave to cool.

4 ▲ Beat the yolks until thick. Beat
in the milk, lime rind and juice and
colouring, if using. Pour into the
pastry case (pie shell) and chill until
set, about 4 hours. To serve, whip the
cream. Pipe a lattice pattern on top.

Fruit Tartlets

MAKES 8

175ml/6fl oz/³/₄ cup redcurrant jelly

15ml/1 tbsp fresh lemon juice

175ml/6fl oz/³/₄ cup whipping cream

675g/1¹/₂lb fresh fruit, such as
strawberries, raspberries, kiwi fruit,
peaches, grapes or currants, peeled
and sliced as necessary

FOR THE PASTRY

150g/5oz/10 tbsp cold butter, cut in pieces

65g/2¹/₂oz/generous ¹/₄ cup soft dark
brown sugar

45ml/3 tbsp unsweetened cocoa powder

200g/7oz/1³/₄ cups plain
(all-purpose) flour

1 egg white

1 For the pastry, combine the butter,
brown sugar and cocoa over low heat.
When the butter is melted, remove
from the heat and sift over the flour.
Stir, then add just enough egg white
to bind the mixture. Gather into a
ball, wrap in clear film (plastic wrap)
and chill for 30 minutes.

2 ▲ Grease eight 7.5cm/3in tartlet tins
(muffin pans). Roll out pastry between
2 sheets of baking parchment. Cut eight
10cm/4in rounds with a fluted cutter.

3 Line the tartlet tins. Prick the
base. Chill for 15 minutes. Preheat
the oven to 180°C/350°F/Gas 4.

4 Bake until firm, 20–25 minutes.
Cool, then remove from the tins.

5 ▲ Melt the jelly with the lemon
juice. Brush a thin layer in the bottom
of the tartlets. Whip the cream and
spread a thin layer in the tartlet cases.
Arrange the fruit on top. Brush with
the glaze and serve.

Lime Tart (top), Fruit Tartlets

Chocolate Lemon Tart

SERVES 8–10

250g/9oz/1¼ cups caster (superfine) sugar

6 eggs

grated rind of 2 lemons

175ml/6fl oz/¾ cup lemon juice

175ml/6fl oz/¾ cup whipping cream

chocolate curls, for decorating

FOR THE CRUST

190g/6½oz/1⅔ cups plain
(all-purpose) flour

30ml/2 tbsp unsweetened cocoa powder

25g/1oz/¼ cup icing (confectioners') sugar

2.5ml/½ tsp salt

115g/4oz/½ cup butter or margarine

15ml/1 tbsp water

1 ▲ Grease a 25cm/10in tart tin (pan).

2 For the crust, sift the flour, cocoa powder, icing sugar and salt into a bowl. Set aside.

3 ▲ Melt the butter and water over a low heat. Pour over the flour mixture and stir with a wooden spoon until the dough is smooth and the flour has absorbed all the liquid.

4 Press the dough evenly over the base and side of the prepared tart tin. Chill the pastry case (pie shell) while preparing the filling.

5 Preheat a baking sheet in a 190°C/375°F/Gas 5 oven.

6 ▲ Whisk the sugar and eggs until the sugar is dissolved. Add the lemon rind and juice, and mix well. Add the cream. Taste the mixture and add more lemon juice or sugar if needed. It should taste tart but also sweet.

7 Pour the filling into the tart shell and bake on the hot sheet until the filling is set, 20–25 minutes. Cool on a rack. When cool, decorate with the chocolate curls.

Lemon Almond Tart

SERVES 8

165g/5¹/₂oz/scant 1 cup whole
   blanched almonds

90g/3¹/₂oz/¹/₂ cup sugar

2 eggs

grated rind and juice of 1¹/₂ lemons

115g/4oz/¹/₂ cup butter, melted

strips of lemon rind, for decorating

FOR THE CRUST

190g/6¹/₂oz/1²/₃ cups plain (all-purpose) flour

15ml/1 tbsp caster (superfine) sugar

2.5ml/¹/₂ tsp salt

2.5ml/¹/₂ tsp baking powder

75g/3oz/6 tbsp cold unsalted (sweet)
   butter, cut into pieces

45–60ml/3–4 tbsp whipping cream

1 For the crust, sift the flour, sugar, salt and baking powder into a bowl. Add the butter and rub in with your fingertips until the mixture resembles coarse breadcrumbs.

2 ▲ With a fork, stir in just enough cream to bind the dough.

3 Gather into a ball and transfer to a lightly floured surface. Roll out the dough about 3mm/¹/₈in thick and carefully transfer to a 23cm/9in tart tin (pan). Trim and prick the base all over with a fork. Chill for at least 20 minutes.

4 Preheat a baking sheet in a 200°C/ 400°F/Gas 6 oven.

5 Line the tart shell with crumpled baking parchment and fill with dried beans. Bake for 12 minutes. Remove the paper and beans and continue baking until golden, 6–8 minutes more. Reduce the oven temperature to 180°C/350°F/Gas 4.

6 ▲ Grind the almonds finely with 15ml/1 tbsp of the sugar in a food processor, blender, or coffee grinder.

7 ▲ Set a mixing bowl over a pan of hot water. Add the eggs and the remaining sugar, and beat with an electric mixer until the mixture is thick enough to leave a ribbon trail when the beaters are lifted.

8 Stir in the lemon rind and juice, butter and ground almonds.

9 Pour into the pastry case (pie shell). Bake until the filling is golden and set, 35 minutes. Decorate with lemon rind.

Lemon Meringue Pie

grated rind and juice of 1 large lemon
250ml/8fl oz/1 cup plus 15ml/1 tbsp cold water
115g/4oz/generous 1/2 cup plus 75g/3oz/ 6 tbsp caster (superfine) sugar
25g/1oz/2 tbsp butter
45ml/3 tbsp cornflour (cornstarch)
3 eggs, separated
pinch of salt
pinch of cream of tartar
FOR THE PASTRY
150g/5oz/11/4 cups plain (all-purpose) flour
2.5ml/1/2 tsp salt
65g/21/2oz/scant 1/2 cup cold white vegetable fat (shortening), cut in pieces
30ml/2 tbsp iced water

1 For the pastry, sift the flour and salt into a bowl. Add the fat and cut in with a pastry blender until the mixture resembles coarse breadcrumbs. With a fork, stir in just enough water to bind the mixture. Gather into a ball.

2 ▲ On a lightly floured surface, roll out the pastry about 3mm/1/8in thick. Transfer to a 23cm/9in pie dish and trim the edge to leave a 2cm/1/2in overhang.

3 ▲ Fold the overhang under and crimp the edge. Chill the pastry case (pie shell) for at least 20 minutes.

4 Preheat oven to 200°C/400°F/Gas 6.

5 ▲ Prick the case all over with a fork. Line with crumpled baking parchment and fill with baking beans. Bake for 12 minutes. Remove the paper and beans and continue baking until golden, 6–8 minutes more.

6 In a pan, combine the lemon rind and juice, 250ml/8fl oz/1 cup of the water, 115g/4oz/generous 1/2 cup of the sugar, and butter. Bring the mixture to the boil.

7 Meanwhile, in a mixing bowl, dissolve the cornflour in the remaining water.

~ VARIATION ~

For Lime Meringue Pie, substitute the grated rind and juice of two medium-size limes for the lemon.

8 ▲ Add the egg yolks to the lemon mixture and return to the boil, whisking continuously until the mixture thickens, about 5 minutes.

9 Cover the surface with baking parchment and leave to cool.

10 ▲ For the meringue, using an electric mixer beat the egg whites with the salt and cream of tartar until they hold stiff peaks. Add the remaining sugar and beat until glossy.

11 ▲ Spoon the lemon mixture into the pastry case and level. Spoon the meringue on top, smoothing it up to the pastry rim to seal. Bake until golden, 12–15 minutes.

Orange Tart

SERVES 8

200g/7oz/1 cup sugar

250ml/8fl oz/1 cup fresh orange juice, strained

2 large navel oranges

165g/5½oz/scant 1 cup whole blanched almonds

50g/2oz/¼ cup butter

1 egg

15ml/1 tbsp plain (all-purpose) flour

45ml/3 tbsp apricot jam

FOR THE CRUST

215g/7½oz/scant 2 cups plain flour

2.5ml/½ tsp salt

50g/2oz/¼ cup cold butter, cut into pieces

40g/1½oz/3 tbsp cold margarine, cut into pieces

45–60ml/3–4 tbsp iced water

1 For the crust, sift the flour and salt into a bowl. Add the butter and margarine and rub in with your fingertips until the mixture resembles coarse breadcrumbs. Stir in just enough water to bind the dough. Gather into a ball, wrap in clear film (plastic wrap), and chill for at least 20 minutes.

2 On a lightly floured surface, roll out the dough 5mm/¼in thick and transfer to an 20cm/8in tart tin (pan). Trim off the overhang. Chill until needed.

3 In a pan, combine 165g/5½oz/generous ¾ cup of the sugar and the orange juice and boil until thick and syrupy, about 10 minutes.

4 ▲ Cut the oranges into 5mm/¼in slices. Do not peel. Add to the syrup. Simmer gently for 10 minutes, or until glazed. Transfer to a rack to dry. When cool, cut in half. Reserve the syrup. Place a baking sheet in the oven and heat to 200°C/400°F/Gas 6.

5 Grind the almonds finely in a food processor, blender or coffee grinder. With an electric mixer, cream the butter and remaining sugar until light and fluffy. Beat in the egg and 30ml/2 tbsp of the orange syrup. Stir in the almonds and flour.

6 Melt the jam over a low heat, then brush over the pastry case (pie shell). Pour in the almond mixture. Bake until set, about 20 minutes. Leave to cool.

7 ▲ Arrange overlapping orange slices on top. Boil the remaining syrup until thick. Brush on top to glaze.

Pumpkin Pie

SERVES 8

450g/1lb cooked or canned pumpkin

250ml/8fl oz/1 cup whipping cream

2 eggs

115g/4oz/½ cup soft dark brown sugar

60ml/4 tbsp golden (light corn) syrup

7.5ml/1½ tsp ground cinnamon

5ml/1 tsp ground ginger

1.5ml/¼ tsp ground cloves

2.5ml/½ tsp salt

FOR THE PASTRY

175g/6oz/1½ cups plain (all-purpose) flour

2.5ml/½ tsp salt

75g/3oz/6 tbsp cold butter, cut into pieces

40g/1½oz/3 tbsp cold white vegetable fat (shortening), cut into pieces

45–60ml/3–4 tbsp iced water

1 For the pastry, sift the flour and salt into a bowl. Cut in the butter and fat until it resembles coarse crumbs. Bind with iced water. Wrap in clear film (plastic wrap) and chill for 20 minutes.

2 Roll out the dough and line a 23cm/9in pie tin (pan). Trim off the overhang. Roll out the trimmings and cut out leaf shapes. Wet the rim of the pastry case (pie shell) with a brush dipped in water.

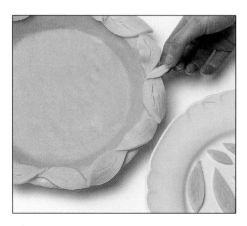

3 ▲ Place the dough leaves around the rim of the pastry case. Chill for about 20 minutes. Preheat the oven to 200°C/400°F/Gas 6.

4 ▲ Line the pastry case with baking parchment. Fill with baking beans and bake for 12 minutes. Remove paper and beans and bake until golden, 6–8 minutes more. Reduce the heat to 190°C/375°F/Gas 5.

5 ▼ Beat together the pumpkin, cream, eggs, sugar, golden syrup, spices and salt. Pour into the pastry case and bake until set, 40 minutes.

Maple Walnut Tart

SERVES 8

3 eggs

pinch of salt

50g/2oz/¼ cup caster (superfine) sugar

50g/2oz/¼ cup butter or margarine, melted

250ml/8fl oz/1 cup pure maple syrup

115g/4oz/1 cup chopped walnuts

whipped cream, for decorating

FOR THE PASTRY

65g/2½oz/9 tbsp plain (all-purpose) flour

65g/2½oz/9 tbsp wholemeal
  (whole-wheat) flour

pinch of salt

50g/2oz/¼ cup cold butter, cut in pieces

40g/1½oz/3 tbsp cold white vegetable fat
  (shortening), cut in pieces

1 egg yolk

30–45ml/2–3 tbsp iced water

1 ▼ For the pastry, mix the flours and salt in a bowl. Add the butter and fat and cut in with a pastry blender until the mixture resembles coarse breadcrumbs. With a fork, stir in the egg yolk and just enough water to bind the pastry. Form into a ball.

2 Wrap in baking parchment and chill for 20 minutes.

3 Preheat oven to 220°C/425°F/Gas 7.

4 On a lightly floured surface, roll out the pastry about 3mm/⅛in thick and transfer to a 23cm/9in pie dish. Trim the edge. To decorate, roll out the trimmings. With a small heart-shaped cutter, stamp out enough hearts to go around the rim of the pie. Brush the edge with water, then arrange the pastry hearts all around.

5 ▲ Prick the bottom with a fork. Line with crumpled baking parchment and fill with baking beans. Bake for 10 minutes. Remove the paper and beans and continue baking until golden brown, 3–6 minutes more.

6 In a bowl, whisk the eggs, salt and sugar together. Stir in the butter and maple syrup.

7 ▲ Set the pastry case (pie shell) on a baking sheet. Pour in the filling, then sprinkle the nuts over the top.

8 Bake until just set, about 35 minutes. Cool on a rack. Decorate with whipped cream, if you like.

Pecan Tart

SERVES 8

3 eggs

pinch of salt

200g/7oz/scant 1 cup soft dark brown sugar

120ml/4fl oz/¹/₂ cup golden
  (light corn) syrup

30ml/2 tbsp fresh lemon juice

75g/3oz/6 tbsp butter, melted

150g/5oz/1¹/₄ cups chopped pecan nuts

50g/2oz/¹/₂ cup pecan halves

FOR THE PASTRY

175g/6oz/1¹/₂ cups plain (all-purpose) flour

15ml/1 tbsp caster (superfine) sugar

5ml/1 tsp baking powder

2.5ml/¹/₂ tsp salt

75g/3oz/6 tbsp cold unsalted (sweet)
  butter, cut in pieces

1 egg yolk

45–60ml/3–4 tbsp whipping cream

1 For the pastry, sift the flour, sugar, baking powder and salt into a bowl. Add the butter and cut in with a pastry blender until the mixture resembles coarse breadcrumbs.

2 ▼ In a bowl, beat together the egg yolk and cream until blended.

~ COOK'S TIP ~

Serve this tart warm, accompanied by ice cream or whipped cream, if you like.

3 ▲ Pour the cream mixture into the flour mixture and stir with a fork.

4 Gather the pastry into a ball. On a lightly floured surface, roll out 3mm/¹/₈in thick and transfer to a 23cm/9in pie dish. Trim the overhang and flute the edge with your fingers. Chill for at least 20 minutes.

5 Preheat a baking sheet in the middle of a 200°C/400°F/Gas 6 oven.

6 In a bowl, lightly whisk the eggs and salt. Add the sugar, syrup, lemon juice and butter. Mix well and stir in the chopped nuts.

7 ▲ Pour into the pastry case (pie shell) and arrange the pecan halves in concentric circles on top.

8 Bake for 10 minutes. Reduce the heat to 170°C/325°F/Gas 3 and continue baking for 25 minutes.

Mince Pies

MAKES 36

175g/6oz/1½ cups finely chopped blanched almonds

150g/5oz/generous ½ cup ready-to-eat dried apricots, finely chopped

175g/6oz/generous 1 cup raisins

150g/5oz/⅔ cup currants

150g/5oz/⅔ cup glacé (candied) cherries, chopped

150g/5oz/¾ cup cut mixed (candied) peel, chopped

115g/4oz/1 cup finely chopped beef suet

grated rind and juice of 2 lemons

grated rind and juice of 1 orange

200g/7oz/scant 1 cup soft dark brown sugar

4 cooking apples, peeled, cored and chopped

10ml/2 tsp ground cinnamon

5ml/1 tsp freshly grated nutmeg

2.5ml/½ tsp ground cloves

250ml/8fl oz/1 cup brandy

225g/8oz/1 cup cream cheese

30ml/2 tbsp caster (superfine) sugar

icing (confectioners') sugar, for dusting

FOR THE PASTRY

425g/15oz/3½ cups plain (all-purpose) flour

150g/5oz/1¼ cups icing (confectioners') sugar

350g/12oz/1½ cups cold butter, cut in pieces

grated rind and juice of 1 orange

milk, for glazing

1 Mix the nuts, dried and preserved fruit, suet, citrus rind and juice, brown sugar, apples and spices.

2 ▲ Stir in the brandy. Cover and leave in a cool place for 2 days.

3 For the pastry, sift the flour and icing sugar into a bowl. Cut in the butter until the mixture resembles coarse breadcrumbs.

4 ▲ Add the orange rind. Stir in just enough orange juice to bind. Gather into a ball, wrap in baking parchment and chill for at least 20 minutes.

5 Preheat the oven to 220°C/425°F/Gas 7. Grease two or three bun trays. Beat together the cream cheese and sugar.

6 ▲ Roll out the pastry 5mm/¼in thick. With a fluted pastry cutter, stamp out 36 8cm/3in rounds.

~ COOK'S TIP ~

The mincemeat mixture may be packed into sterilized jars and sealed. It will keep refrigerated for several months. Add a few tablespoonfuls to give apple pies a lift, or make small mincemeat-filled parcels using filo pastry.

7 ▲ Transfer the rounds to the bun tray. Fill halfway with mincemeat. Top with a teaspoonful of the cream cheese mixture.

8 ▲ Roll out the remaining pastry and stamp out 36 5cm/2in rounds with a fluted cutter. Brush the edges of the pies with milk, then set the rounds on top. Cut a small steam vent in the top of each pie.

9 ▲ Brush lightly with milk. Bake until golden, 15–20 minutes. Leave to cool for 10 minutes before turning out. Dust with icing sugar, if you like.

Shoofly Pie

SERVES 8

115g/4oz/1 cup plain (all-purpose) flour

115g/4oz/1 cup soft dark brown sugar

1.5ml/¼ tsp each salt, ground ginger, cinnamon, mace and grated nutmeg

75g/3oz/6 tbsp cold butter, cut into pieces

2 eggs

120ml/4fl oz/½ cup molasses

120ml/4fl oz/½ cup boiling water

2.5ml/½ tsp bicarbonate of soda (baking soda)

FOR THE PASTRY

115g/4oz/½ cup cream cheese, at room temperature, cut into pieces

115g/4oz/½ cup cold butter, at room temperature, cut into pieces

115g/4oz/1 cup plain flour

1 For the pastry, put the cream cheese and butter in a mixing bowl. Sift over the flour.

2 ▲ Cut in with a pastry blender until the dough just holds together. Wrap in clear film (plastic wrap) and chill for at least 30 minutes.

3 Put a baking sheet in the centre of the oven and preheat the oven to 190°C/375°F/Gas 5.

4 In a bowl, mix the flour, sugar, salt and spices. Rub in the butter with your fingertips until the mixture resembles coarse crumbs. Set aside.

5 On a lightly floured surface, roll out the dough and line a 23cm/9in pie tin (pan). Trim the overhanging pastry and flute the rim.

6 ▲ Spoon a third of the crumbed mixture into the pastry case (pie shell).

7 ▲ To complete the filling, whisk the eggs with the molasses in a large bowl until combined.

8 Pour the boiling water into a small bowl. Stir in the bicarbonate of soda; the mixture will foam. Immediately whisk into the egg mixture. Pour carefully into the pastry case and sprinkle the remaining crumbed mixture evenly over the top.

9 Stand on the hot baking sheet and bake until browned, about 35 minutes. Leave to cool to room temperature, then serve.

Treacle Tart

SERVES 4–6

175ml/6fl oz/³/₄ cup golden (light corn) syrup
75g/3oz/1¹/₂ cups fresh white breadcrumbs
grated rind of 1 lemon
30ml/2 tbsp lemon juice
FOR THE PASTRY
175g/6oz/1¹/₂ cups plain (all-purpose) flour
2.5ml/¹/₂ tsp salt
75g/3oz/6 tbsp cold butter, cut in pieces
40g/1¹/₂oz/3 tbsp cold margarine, cut in pieces
45–60ml/3–4 tbsp iced water

1 For the pastry, combine the flour and salt in a bowl. Add the butter and margarine, and cut in with a pastry blender until the mixture resembles coarse breadcrumbs.

2 ▲ With a fork, stir in just enough water to bind the pastry. Gather into a ball, wrap in clear film (plastic wrap) and chill for at least 20 minutes.

3 On a lightly floured surface, roll out the pastry to a thickness of 3mm/¹/₈in. Transfer to an 20cm/8in pie dish and trim off the overhang. Chill for at least 20 minutes. Reserve the trimmings for the lattice top.

4 Preheat a baking sheet at the top of a 200°C/400°F/Gas 6 oven.

5 In a pan, warm the syrup until thin and runny.

6 ▲ Remove from the heat and stir in the breadcrumbs and lemon rind. Leave for 10 minutes so that the bread can absorb the syrup. Add more breadcrumbs if the mixture is thin. Stir in the lemon juice and spread evenly in the pastry case (pie shell).

7 Roll out the pastry trimmings and cut into 10–12 thin strips.

8 ▼ Lay half the strips on the filling, then lay the remaining strips at an angle over them to form a lattice.

9 Place on the hot sheet and bake for 10 minutes. Lower the heat to 190°C/375°F/Gas 5. Bake until golden, about 15 minutes more. Serve warm or cold.

Chess Pie

SERVES 8

2 eggs
45ml/3 tbsp whipping cream
115g/4oz/¹/₂ cup soft dark brown sugar
30ml/2 tbsp granulated sugar
30ml/2 tbsp plain (all-purpose) flour
15ml/1 tbsp whisky
40g/1¹/₂oz/3 tbsp butter, melted
50g/2oz/¹/₂ cup chopped walnuts
75g/3oz/¹/₂ cup pitted dates, chopped
whipped cream, for serving
FOR THE PASTRY
75g/3oz/6 tbsp cold butter
40g/1¹/₂oz/3 tbsp cold vegetable fat
175g/6oz/1¹/₂ cups plain flour
2.5ml/¹/₂ tsp salt
45–60ml/3–4 tbsp iced water

1 ▲ For the pastry, cut the butter and fat into small pieces.

2 Sift the flour and salt into a bowl. With a pastry blender, cut in the butter and fat until the mixture resembles coarse crumbs. Stir in just enough water to bind. Gather into a ball, wrap in baking parchment and chill for at least 20 minutes.

3 Place a baking sheet in the oven and preheat it to 190°C/375°F/Gas 5.

4 Roll out the dough thinly and line a 23cm/9in pie tin (pan). Trim the edge. Roll out the trimmings, cut thin strips and braid them. Brush the edge of the pastry case (pie shell) with water and fit the pastry braids around the rim.

5 ▲ In a mixing bowl, whisk together the eggs and cream.

6 Add both sugars and beat until well combined. Sift over 15ml/1 tbsp of the flour and stir in. Add the whisky, the melted butter and the walnuts. Stir to combine.

7 ▲ Mix the dates with the remaining flour and stir into the walnut mixture.

8 Pour into the pastry case and bake until the pastry is golden and the filling puffed up, about 35 minutes. Serve at room temperature, with whipped cream, if you like.

Coconut Cream Tart

SERVES 8

150g/5oz/scant 1¹/₂ cups desiccated (dry unsweetened) coconut

150g/5oz/³/₄ cup caster (superfine) sugar

60ml/4 tbsp cornflour (cornstarch)

pinch of salt

600ml/1 pint/2¹/₂ cups milk

50ml/2fl oz/¹/₄ cup whipping cream

2 egg yolks

25g/1oz/2 tbsp unsalted (sweet) butter

10ml/2 tsp vanilla extract

FOR THE PASTRY

150g/5oz/1¹/₄ cups plain (all-purpose) flour

1.5ml/¹/₄ tsp salt

40g/1¹/₂oz/3 tbsp cold butter, cut in pieces

25g/1oz/2 tbsp cold white vegetable fat (shortening)

30–45ml/2–3 tbsp iced water

1 For the pastry, sift the flour and salt, then cut in the butter and fat until it resembles coarse breadcrumbs.

2 ▲ With a fork, stir in just enough water to bind the pastry. Gather into a ball, wrap in baking parchment and chill for 20 minutes.

3 Preheat the oven to 220°C/425°F/Gas 7. Roll out the pastry 3mm/¹/₈in thick. Line a 23cm/9in pie dish. Trim and flute the edges. Prick the base. Line with baking parchment and fill with baking beans. Bake for 10–12 minutes. Remove paper and beans, reduce heat to 180°C/350°F/Gas 4 and bake until brown, 10–15 minutes.

4 ▲ Spread 50g/2oz of the coconut on a baking sheet and toast in the oven until golden, 6–8 minutes, stirring often. Set aside for decorating.

5 Put the sugar, cornflour and salt in a pan. In a bowl, whisk the milk, cream and egg yolks. Add the egg mixture to the pan.

6 ▼ Cook over a low heat, stirring, until the mixture comes to the boil. Boil for 1 minute, then remove from the heat. Add the butter, vanilla and remaining coconut.

7 Pour into the prebaked pastry case (pie shell). When cool, sprinkle toasted coconut in a ring in the centre.

Black Bottom Pie

SERVES 8

10ml/2 tsp gelatine
45ml/3 tbsp cold water
2 eggs, separated
150g/5oz/1¼ cups caster (superfine) sugar
15g/½oz/2 tbsp cornflour (cornstarch)
2.5ml/½ tsp salt
475ml/16fl oz/2 cups milk
50g/2oz plain (semisweet) chocolate, finely chopped
30ml/2 tbsp rum
1.5ml/¼ tsp cream of tartar
chocolate curls, for decorating
FOR THE CRUST
175g/6oz/3 cups gingersnaps, crushed
65g/2½oz/5 tbsp butter, melted

1 Preheat the oven to 180°C/350°F/ Gas 4.

2 For the crust, mix the crushed gingersnaps and melted butter.

3 ▲ Press the mixture evenly over the bottom and side of a 23cm/9in pie plate. Bake for 6 minutes.

4 Sprinkle the gelatine over the water and leave to soften.

5 Beat the egg yolks in a large mixing bowl and set aside.

6 In a pan, combine half the sugar, the cornflour and salt. Gradually stir in the milk. Boil for 1 minute, stirring constantly.

7 ▲ Whisk the hot milk mixture into the yolks, then pour all back into the pan and return to the boil, whisking. Cook for 1 minute, still whisking. Remove from the heat.

8 ▲ Measure out 225g/8oz of the hot custard mixture and pour into a bowl. Add the chopped chocolate to the bowl, and stir until melted. Stir in half the rum and pour into the pastry case (pie shell).

9 ▲ Whisk the softened gelatine into the plain custard until it has dissolved, then stir in the remaining rum. Set the pan in cold water until it reaches room temperature.

10 ▲ With an electric mixer, beat the egg whites and cream of tartar until they hold stiff peaks. Add the remaining sugar gradually, beating or whisking thoroughly at each addition.

11 ▲ Fold the custard into the egg whites, then spoon over the chocolate mixture in the pastry case. Chill until set, about 2 hours.

12 Decorate the top with chocolate curls. Keep the pie chilled until ready to serve.

~ COOK'S TIP ~

To make chocolate curls, melt 225g/8oz plain chocolate over hot water, stir in 15ml/1 tbsp white vegetable fat (shortening) and mould in a small foil-lined loaf tin (pan). For large curls, soften the bar between your hands and scrape off curls from the wide side with a vegetable peeler; for small curls, grate from the narrow side using a box grater.

Velvety Mocha Tart

10ml/2 tsp instant espresso coffee
30ml/2 tbsp hot water
350ml/12fl oz/1¹/₂ cups whipping cream
175g/6oz plain (semisweet) chocolate
25g/1oz dark (bittersweet) cooking chocolate
120ml/4fl oz/¹/₂ cup whipped cream, for decorating
chocolate-covered coffee beans, for decorating
FOR THE BASE
150g/5oz/2¹/₂ cups chocolate wafers, crushed
30ml/2 tbsp caster (superfine) sugar
65g/2¹/₂oz/5 tbsp butter, melted

1 ▲ For the base, mix the crushed chocolate wafers and sugar together, then stir in the melted butter.

2 Press the mixture evenly over the base and sides of a 23cm/9in pie dish. Chill until firm.

3 In a bowl, dissolve the coffee in the water and set aside.

4 Pour the cream into a mixing bowl. Set the bowl in hot water to warm the cream, bringing it closer to the temperature of the chocolate.

5 Melt both the chocolates in the top of a double boiler, or in a heatproof bowl set over a pan of hot water. Remove from the heat when nearly melted and stir to continue melting. Set the base of the pan in cool water to reduce the temperature. Be careful not to splash any water on the chocolate or it will become grainy.

6 ▲ With an electric mixer, whip the cream until it is lightly fluffy. Add the dissolved coffee and whip until the cream just holds its shape.

7 ▲ When the chocolate is at room temperature, fold it gently into the cream with a large metal spoon.

8 Pour into the chilled biscuit base and chill until firm. To serve, pipe a ring of whipped cream rosettes around the edge, then place a chocolate-covered coffee bean in the centre of each rosette.

Brandy Alexander Tart

SERVES 8

120ml/4fl oz/^{1}/$_2$ cup cold water
15ml/1 tbsp powdered gelatine
115g/4oz/generous ^{1}/$_2$ cup caster (superfine) sugar
3 eggs, separated
60ml/4 tbsp brandy
60ml/4 tbsp crème de cacao
pinch of salt
300ml/^{1}/$_2$ pint/1^1/$_4$ cups whipping cream
chocolate curls, for decorating
FOR THE BISCUIT CRUST
225g/8oz/4cups digestive biscuits (graham crackers), crumbed
65g/2^1/$_2$oz/5 tbsp butter, melted
15ml/1 tbsp caster sugar

1 Preheat oven to 190°C/375°F/ Gas 5.

2 For the crust, mix the biscuit crumbs with the butter and sugar in a bowl.

3 ▲ Press the crumbs evenly on to the base and sides of a 23cm/9in tart tin (pan). Bake until just brown, about 10 minutes. Cool on a rack.

4 Place the water in the top of a double boiler set over hot water. Sprinkle over the powdered gelatine and leave to stand for 5 minutes to soften. Add half the sugar and the egg yolks. Whisk constantly over a very low heat until the gelatine dissolves and the mixture has thickened slightly. Do not allow the mixture to boil.

5 ▲ Remove from the heat and stir in the brandy and crème de cacao.

6 Set the pan over iced water and stir occasionally until it cools and thickens; it should not set firmly.

7 With an electric mixer, beat the egg whites and salt until they hold stiff peaks. Beat in the remaining sugar. Spoon a dollop of whites into the yolk mixture and fold in to lighten.

8 ▼ Pour the egg yolk mixture over the remaining whites and fold together.

9 Whip the cream until soft peaks form, then gently fold into the filling. Spoon into the baked biscuit case and chill until set, 3–4 hours. Decorate the top with chocolate curls before serving.

Candied Fruit Pie

SERVES 10

15ml/1 tbsp rum

50g/2oz/¼ cup mixed glacé (candied) fruit, chopped

450ml/¾ pint/scant 2 cups milk

20ml/4 tsp gelatine

90g/3½oz/½ cup caster (superfine) sugar

2.5ml/½ tsp salt

3 eggs, separated

250ml/8fl oz/1 cup whipping cream

chocolate curls, for decorating

FOR THE CRUST

175g/6oz/3 cups digestive biscuits (graham crackers), crushed

65g/2½oz/5 tbsp butter, melted

15ml/1 tbsp sugar

1 For the crust, mix the crushed digestive biscuits, butter and sugar. Press evenly and firmly over the base and side of a 23cm/9in pie plate. Chill until firm.

2 ▲ In a bowl, stir together the rum and glacé fruit. Set aside.

3 Pour 120ml/4fl oz/½ cup of the milk into a bowl. Sprinkle over the gelatine. Leave to soften for 5 minutes.

4 ▲ In the top of a double boiler, combine 50g/2oz/¼ cup of the sugar, the remaining milk and salt. Stir in the gelatine mixture. Cook over hot water, stirring, until the gelatine dissolves.

5 Whisk in the egg yolks and cook, stirring, until thick enough to coat a spoon. Do not boil. Pour the custard over the glacé fruit mixture. Set in a bowl of iced water to cool. Whip the cream lightly. Set aside.

6 With an electric mixer, beat the egg whites until they hold soft peaks. Add the remaining sugar and beat just enough to blend. Fold in a large dollop of the egg whites into the cooled gelatine mixture. Pour into the remaining egg whites and carefully fold together. Fold in the cream.

7 ▲ Pour into the biscuit base and chill until firm. Decorate the top with chocolate curls.

Chocolate Chiffon Pie

SERVES 8

200g/7oz plain (semisweet) chocolate

250ml/8fl oz/1 cup milk

15ml/1 tbsp gelatine

90g/3¹/₂oz/¹/₂ cup sugar

2 large (US extra-large) eggs, separated

5ml/1 tsp vanilla extract

350ml/12fl oz/1¹/₂ cups whipping cream

pinch of salt

whipped cream and chocolate curls,
    for decorating

FOR THE CRUST

200g/7oz/3¹/₂ cups digestive biscuits
    (graham crackers), crushed

75g/3oz/6 tbsp butter, melted

1 Place a baking sheet in the oven and preheat to 180°C/350°F/Gas 4.

2 For the crust, mix the crushed digestive biscuits and butter in a bowl. Press evenly over the base and side of a 23cm/9in pie plate. Bake for 8 minutes. Leave to cool.

3 Chop the chocolate, then grate in a food processor or blender. Set aside.

4 Place the milk in the top of a double boiler. Sprinkle over the gelatine. Leave to stand for 5 minutes to soften.

5 ▲ Set the top of a double boiler over hot water. Add 40g/1¹/₂oz/3 tbsp sugar, the chocolate and the egg yolks. Stir until dissolved. Add the vanilla extract.

6 ▲ Set the top of the double boiler in a bowl of ice and stir until the mixture reaches room temperature. Remove from the ice and set aside.

7 Whip the cream lightly. Set aside. With an electric mixer, beat the egg whites and salt until they hold soft peaks. Add the remaining sugar and beat only enough to blend.

8 Fold a dollop of egg whites into the chocolate mixture, then pour back into the whites and fold in.

9 ▲ Fold in the whipped cream and pour into the biscuit base. Put in the freezer until just set, about 5 minutes. If the centre sinks, fill with any remaining mixture. Chill for 3–4 hours. Decorate with whipped cream and chocolate curls. Serve cold.

Chocolate Cheesecake Tart

SERVES 8

350g/12oz/1¹/₂ cups cream cheese

60ml/4 tbsp whipping cream

225g/8oz/generous 1 cup caster (superfine) sugar

50g/2oz/¹/₂ cup unsweetened cocoa powder

2.5ml/¹/₂ tsp ground cinnamon

3 eggs

whipped cream, for decorating

chocolate curls, for decorating

FOR THE BASE

75g/3oz/1¹/₂ cups digestive biscuits (graham crackers), crushed

40g/1¹/₂oz/³/₄ cup crushed amaretti biscuits (if unavailable, use extra crushed digestive biscuits)

75g/3oz/6 tbsp butter, melted

1 Preheat a baking sheet in the centre of a 180°C/350°F/Gas 4 oven.

2 For the base, mix the crushed biscuits and butter in a bowl.

3 ▲ With a spoon, press the mixture over the base and sides of a 23cm/9in pie dish. Bake for 8 minutes. Leave to cool. Keep the oven on.

4 With an electric mixer, beat the cheese and cream together until smooth. Beat in the sugar, cocoa and cinnamon until blended.

5 ▼ Add the eggs, one at a time, beating just enough to blend.

6 Pour into the biscuit base and bake on the hot sheet for 25–30 minutes. The filling will sink down as it cools. Decorate with whipped cream and chocolate curls.

Frozen Strawberry Tart

SERVES 8

225g/8oz/1 cup cream cheese

250ml/8fl oz/1 cup sour cream

500g/1¹/₄lb/5 cups frozen strawberries, thawed and sliced

FOR THE BASE

115g/4oz/2 cups digestive biscuits (graham crackers), crushed

15ml/1 tbsp caster (superfine) sugar

70g/2¹/₂oz/5 tbsp butter, melted

~ VARIATION ~

For Frozen Raspberry Tart, use raspberries in place of the strawberries, and prepare the same way, or try other frozen fruit.

1 ▲ For the base, mix together the biscuits, sugar and butter.

2 Press the mixture evenly and firmly over the base and sides of a 23cm/9in pie dish. Freeze until firm.

3 ▼ Blend together the cream cheese and sour cream. Reserve 90ml/6 tbsp of the strawberries. Add the remainder to the cream cheese mixture.

4 Pour the filling into the biscuit base and freeze for 6–8 hours until firm. To serve, spoon some of the reserved berries and juice on top.

Chocolate Cheesecake Pie (top), Frozen Strawberry Tart

Kiwi Ricotta Cheese Tart

SERVES 8

75g/3oz/¹/₂ cup blanched almonds, ground

90g/3¹/₂oz/¹/₂ cup caster (superfine) sugar

900g/2lb/4 cups ricotta cheese

250ml/8fl oz/1 cup whipping cream

1 egg and 3 egg yolks

15ml/1 tbsp plain (all-purpose) flour

pinch of salt

30ml/2 tbsp rum

grated rind of 1 lemon

40ml/2¹/₂ tbsp lemon juice

30ml/2 tbsp honey

5 kiwi fruit

FOR THE PASTRY

150g/5oz/1¹/₄ cups plain (all-purpose) flour

15ml/1 tbsp caster (superfine) sugar

2.5ml/¹/₂ tsp salt

2.5ml/¹/₂ tsp baking powder

75g/3oz/6 tbsp butter

1 egg yolk

45–60ml/3–4 tbsp whipping cream

1 For the pastry, mix together the flour, sugar, salt and baking powder in a large bowl. Cut the butter into cubes and gradually rub it into the pastry mixture. Mix together the egg yolk and cream. Stir in just enough to bind the pastry.

2 ▲ Transfer to a lightly floured surface, flatten slightly, wrap and chill for 30 minutes. Preheat the oven to 220°C/425°F/Gas 7.

3 ▲ On a lightly floured surface, roll out the dough to 3mm/¹/₈in thickness. Transfer to a 23cm/9in springform tart tin (pan). Crimp the edge.

4 ▲ Prick the pastry with a fork. Line with baking parchment and fill with dried beans. Bake for 10 minutes. Remove the paper and beans and bake for 6–8 minutes more until golden. Leave to cool. Reduce the temperature to 180°C/350°F/Gas 4.

5 ▲ Mix the almonds with 15ml/ 1 tbsp of the sugar in a food processor or blender.

6 Beat the ricotta until creamy. Add the cream, egg, yolks, remaining sugar, flour, salt, rum, lemon rind and 30ml/ 2 tbsp of lemon juice. Combine.

7 ▲ Stir in the ground almonds until well blended.

8 Pour into a pastry case (pie shell) and bake for 1 hour. Chill, loosely covered for 2–3 hours. Turn out on to a plate.

9 Combine the honey and remaining lemon juice for the glaze.

10 ▲ Peel the kiwi fruits. Halve them lengthways, then slice. Arrange the slices in rows across the top of the tart. Just before serving, brush with the honey glaze.

Apple Strudel

SERVES 10–12

75g/3oz/generous ¹/₂ cup raisins
30ml/2 tbsp brandy
5 eating apples, such as Granny Smith or Cox's
3 large cooking apples
90g/3¹/₂oz/scant ¹/₂ cup soft dark brown sugar
5ml/1 tsp ground cinnamon
grated rind and juice of 1 lemon
25g/1oz/¹/₂ cup dry breadcrumbs
50g/2oz/¹/₂ cup chopped pecan nuts or walnuts
12 sheets frozen filo pastry, thawed if frozen
175g/6oz/³/₄ cup butter, melted
icing (confectioners') sugar, for dusting

1 Soak the raisins in the brandy for at least 15 minutes.

2 ▼ Peel, core and thinly slice the apples. In a bowl, combine the sugar, cinnamon and lemon rind. Stir in the apples and half the breadcrumbs.

3 Add the raisins, nuts and lemon juice, and stir until blended.

4 Preheat the oven to 190°C/375°F/ Gas 5. Grease two baking sheets.

5 ▲ Carefully unfold the filo sheets. Keep the unused sheets covered with baking parchment. Lift off one sheet, place on a clean surface and brush with melted butter. Lay a second sheet on top and brush with butter. Continue until you have a stack of six buttered sheets.

6 Sprinkle a few tablespoons of breadcrumbs over the last sheet and spoon half the apple mixture along the bottom edge of the strip.

7 ▲ Starting at the apple-filled end, roll up the pastry, as for a Swiss roll tin (jelly roll pan). Place on a baking sheet, seam-side down, and carefully fold under the ends to seal. Repeat the procedure to make a second strudel. Brush both with butter.

8 Bake the strudels for 45 minutes. Leave to cool slightly. Using a small sieve (strainer), dust with a fine layer of icing sugar. Serve warm.

Cherry Strudel

SERVES 8

65g/2¹/₂oz/generous 1 cup fresh breadcrumbs
175g/6oz/³/₄ cup butter, melted
200g/7oz/1 cup caster (superfine) sugar
15ml/1 tbsp ground cinnamon
5ml/1 tsp grated lemon rind
450g/1lb sour cherries, pitted
8 sheets filo pastry, thawed if frozen
icing (confectioners') sugar, for dusting

1 In a frying pan, lightly fry the fresh breadcrumbs in 65g/2¹/₂oz of the melted butter until golden. Set aside to cool.

2 ▲ In a large mixing bowl, toss together the sugar, cinnamon and lemon rind.

3 Stir in the cherries.

4 Preheat the oven to 190°C/375°F/ Gas 5. Grease a baking sheet.

5 Carefully unfold the filo sheets. Keep the unused sheets covered with damp kitchen paper. Lift off one sheet, place on a flat surface lined with baking parchment. Brush the pastry with melted butter. Sprinkle about an eighth of the breadcrumbs evenly over the surface.

6 ▲ Lay a second sheet of filo on top, brush with butter and sprinkle with crumbs. Continue until you have a stack of eight buttered, crumbed sheets.

7 Spoon the cherry mixture along the bottom edge of the strip. Starting at the cherry-filled end, roll up the dough as for a Swiss roll tin (jelly roll pan). Use the paper to help flip the strudel on to the baking sheet, seam-side down.

8 ▼ Carefully fold under the ends to seal in the fruit. Brush the top with any remaining butter.

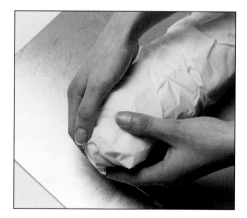

9 Bake the strudel for 45 minutes. Leave to cool slightly. Using a small sieve (strainer), dust with a fine layer of icing sugar.

Mushroom Quiche

SERVES 8

450g/1lb/6 cups mushrooms

30ml/2 tbsp olive oil

15ml/1 tbsp butter

1 clove garlic, finely chopped

15ml/1 tbsp lemon juice

30ml/2 tbsp finely chopped fresh parsley

3 eggs

350ml/12fl oz/1½ cups whipping cream

65g/2½oz/¾ cup freshly grated Parmesan cheese

salt and ground black pepper

FOR THE CRUST

190g/6½oz/1⅔ cups plain (all-purpose) flour

2.5ml/½ tsp salt

75g/3oz cold butter, cut into pieces

50g/2oz/¼ cup cold margarine, cut into pieces

45–60ml/3–4 tbsp iced water

1 For the crust, sift the flour and salt. Rub in the butter and margarine until it resembles coarse breadcrumbs. Stir in enough water to bind.

2 Gather into a ball, wrap in clear film (plastic wrap) and chill for 20 minutes.

3 Preheat a baking sheet in a 190°C/375°F/Gas 5 oven.

4 Roll out the dough 3mm/⅛in thick. Transfer to a 23cm/9in quiche tin (pan) and trim. Prick the base all over with a fork. Line with baking parchment and fill with dried beans. Bake for 12 minutes. Remove the paper and beans and continue baking until golden, about 5 minutes more.

5 ▲ Wipe the mushrooms with damp kitchen paper to remove any dirt. Trim the ends of the stalks, place on a cutting board, and slice thinly.

6 Heat the oil and butter in a frying pan. Stir in the mushrooms, garlic and lemon juice. Season with salt and pepper. Cook until the mushrooms render their liquid, then raise the heat and cook until dry.

7 ▼ Stir in the parsley and add more salt and pepper if necessary.

8 Whisk the eggs and cream together, then stir in the mushrooms. Sprinkle the cheese over the base of the prebaked pastry case (pie shell) and pour the mushroom filling over the top.

9 Bake until puffed and brown, about 30 minutes. Serve the quiche warm.

Bacon and Cheese Quiche

SERVES 8

115g/4oz medium-thick bacon slices

3 eggs

350ml/12fl oz/1½ cups whipping cream

90g/3½oz Gruyère cheese, grated

pinch of freshly grated nutmeg

salt and ground black pepper

FOR THE CRUST

190g/6½oz/1⅔ cups plain (all-purpose) flour

2.5ml/½ tsp salt

75g/3oz/6 tbsp cold butter, cut into pieces

40g/1½oz/3 tbsp cold margarine, cut into pieces

45–60ml/3–4 tbsp iced water

1 Make the crust as per steps 1–4 above. Keep the oven at 190°C/375°F/Gas 5.

2 ▲ Fry the bacon until crisp. Drain, then crumble into small pieces. Sprinkle in the pastry case (pie shell).

3 ▲ Beat together the eggs, cream, cheese, nutmeg, salt and pepper. Pour over the bacon and bake until puffed and brown, about 30 minutes. Serve the quiche warm.

Mushroom Quiche (top), Bacon and Cheese Quiche

Cheese and Tomato Quiche

SERVES 6–8

10 medium tomatoes

1 × 50g/2oz can anchovy fillets, drained and finely chopped

120ml/4fl oz/¹/₂ cup whipping cream

200g/7oz/1³/₄ cups mature Cheddar cheese, grated

25g/1oz/¹/₂ cup wholemeal (whole-wheat) breadcrumbs

2.5ml/¹/₂ tsp dried thyme

salt and ground black pepper

FOR THE CRUST

215g/7¹/₂oz/scant 2 cups plain (all-purpose) flour

115g/4oz/¹/₂ cup cold butter, cut into pieces

1 egg yolk

30–45ml/2–3 tbsp iced water

1 Preheat oven to 200°C/400°F/ Gas 6.

2 For the crust, sift the flour and ¹/₂ tsp salt into a bowl. Rub in the butter with your fingertips until the mixture resembles coarse breadcrumbs.

3 ▲ With a fork, stir in the egg yolk and enough water to bind the dough.

4 Roll out the dough to about 3mm/¹/₈in thick and transfer to a 23cm/9in quiche tin (pan). Chill the dough until needed.

5 ▲ Score the bottoms of the tomatoes. Plunge in boiling water for 1 minute. Remove and peel off the skin with a knife. Cut in quarters and remove the seeds with a spoon.

6 ▲ In a bowl, mix the anchovies and cream. Stir in the cheese.

7 Sprinkle the breadcrumbs in the crust. Arrange the tomatoes on top. Season with thyme, salt and pepper.

8 ▲ Spoon the cheese mixture on top. Bake until golden, 25–30 minutes. Serve warm.

Onion and Anchovy Tart

SERVES 8

60ml/4 tbsp olive oil

900g/2lb onions, sliced

5ml/1 tsp dried thyme

2–3 tomatoes, sliced

24 small black olives, pitted

1 × 50g/2oz can anchovy fillets, drained and sliced

6 sun-dried tomatoes, cut into slivers

salt and ground black pepper

FOR THE CRUST

190g/6½oz/1⅔ cups plain (all-purpose) flour

2.5ml/½ tsp salt

115g/4oz/½ cup cold butter, cut into pieces

1 egg yolk

30–45ml/2–3 tbsp iced water

1 ▲ For the crust, sift the flour and salt into a bowl. Rub in the butter with your fingertips until the mixture resembles coarse breadcrumbs. Stir in the yolk and enough water to bind.

2 ▲ Roll out the dough to a thickness of about 3mm/⅛in. Transfer to a 23cm/9in quiche tin (pan) and trim the edge. Chill in the refrigerator until needed.

3 ▲ Heat the oil in a frying pan. Add the onions, thyme and seasoning. Cook over low heat, covered, for 25 minutes. Uncover and continue cooking until soft. Cool. Preheat the oven to 200°C/400°F/Gas 6.

4 ▼ Spoon the onions into the pastry case (pie shell) and top with the tomato slices. Arrange the olives in rows. Make a lattice pattern, alternating lines of anchovies and sun-dried tomatoes. Bake until golden, 20–25 minutes.

Ricotta and Basil Tart

SERVES 8–10

50g/2oz/2 cups basil leaves

25g/1oz/1 cup flat-leaf parsley

120ml/4fl oz/½ cup extra-virgin olive oil

2 eggs

1 egg yolk

800g/1¾lb/3½ cups ricotta cheese

90g/3½oz/scant 1 cup black olives, pitted

65g/2½oz/¾ cup freshly grated
   Parmesan cheese

salt and ground black pepper

FOR THE CRUST

190g/6½oz/1⅔ cups plain
   (all-purpose) flour

2.5ml/½ tsp salt

75g/3oz/6 tbsp cold butter, cut into pieces

40g/1½oz/3 tbsp cold margarine,
   cut into pieces

45–60ml/3–4 tbsp iced water

1 ▲ For the crust, combine the flour and salt in a bowl. Add the butter and margarine.

2 Rub in with your fingertips until the mixture resembles coarse breadcrumbs. With a fork, stir in just enough water to bind the dough. Gather into a ball, wrap in clear film (plastic wrap), and chill for 20 minutes.

3 Preheat a baking sheet in a 190°C/375°F/Gas 5 oven.

4 Roll out the dough 3mm/⅛in thick and transfer to a 25cm/10in quiche tin (pan). Prick the base with a fork and line with baking parchment. Fill with dried beans and bake for 12 minutes. Remove the paper and beans and bake until golden, 3–5 minutes more. Lower the heat to 180°C/350°F/Gas 4.

5 ▲ In a food processor or blender, combine the basil, parsley and olive oil. Season well with salt and pepper and process until finely chopped.

6 In a bowl, whisk the eggs and yolk to blend. Gently fold in the ricotta.

7 ▲ Fold in the basil mixture and olives until well combined. Stir in the Parmesan and adjust the seasoning.

8 Pour into the prebaked pastry case (pie shell) and bake until set, about 30–35 minutes.

Pennsylvania Dutch Ham and Apple Pie

SERVES 6–8

5 tart cooking apples
60ml/4 tbsp soft light brown sugar
15ml/1 tbsp plain (all-purpose) flour
pinch of ground cloves
pinch of ground black pepper
175g/6oz sliced cooked ham
25g/1oz/2 tbsp butter or margarine
60ml/4 tbsp whipping cream
1 egg yolk
FOR THE PASTRY
225g/8oz/2 cups plain (all-purpose) flour
2.5ml/¹⁄₂ tsp salt
75g/3oz/6 tbsp cold butter, cut into pieces
50g/2oz/¹⁄₄ cup cold margarine, cut into pieces
60–120ml/4–8 tbsp iced water

1 For the pastry, sift the flour and salt into a large bowl. Rub in the butter and margarine until the mixture resembles coarse crumbs. Stir in enough water to bind together, gather into two balls, and wrap in clear film (plastic wrap). Chill for 20 minutes. Preheat the oven to 220°C/425°F/Gas 7.

2 ▲ Quarter, core, peel and thinly slice the apples. Place in a bowl and toss with the sugar, flour, cloves and pepper to coat evenly. Set aside.

3 Roll out one dough ball thinly and line a 25cm/10in pie tin (pan), letting the excess pastry hang over the edge.

4 Arrange half the ham slices in the bottom of the pastry case. Top with a ring of spiced apple slices, then dot with half the butter or margarine.

5 ▲ Repeat the layers, finishing with apples. Dot with butter or margarine. Pour over 45ml/3 tbsp of the cream.

6 Roll out the remaining pastry to make a lid. Place it on top, fold the top edge under the bottom and press.

7 ▲ Roll out the pastry scraps and cut out decorative shapes. Arrange on top of the pie. Scallop the edge, using your fingers and a fork. Cut steam vents. Mix the egg yolk and remaining cream and brush on top to glaze.

8 Bake for 10 minutes. Reduce the heat to 180°C/350°F/Gas 4 and bake until golden, 30–35 minutes more. Serve hot.

CAKES & GATEAUX

AS DELICIOUS AS THEY ARE
BEAUTIFUL, THESE CAKES AND
GATEAUX ARE PERFECT TO SERVE
AT TEATIME OR FOR DESSERT.
DELIGHTFUL PARTY CAKES MAKE
SPECIAL OCCASIONS MEMORABLE.

Angel Cake

SERVES 12–14

130g/4¹/₂oz/generous 1 cup sifted plain (all-purpose) flour
30ml/2 tbsp cornflour (cornstarch)
300g/11oz/generous 1¹/₂ cups caster (superfine) sugar
275–300g/10–11oz egg whites (about 10–11 eggs)
6.5ml/1¹/₄ tsp cream of tartar
1.5ml/¹/₄ tsp salt
5ml/1 tsp vanilla extract
1.5ml/¹/₄ tsp almond extract
icing (confectioners') sugar, for dusting

1 Preheat the oven to 160°C/325°F/ Gas 3.

2 ▼ Sift the flours before measuring, then sift them four times with 90g/ 3¹/₂oz/¹/₂ cup of the sugar.

3 With an electric mixer, beat the egg whites until foamy. Sift over the cream of tartar and salt, and continue to beat until the whites hold soft peaks when the beaters are lifted.

4 ▲ Add the remaining sugar in three batches, beating well after each addition. Stir in the vanilla and almond extracts.

5 ▲ Add the flour mixture, in two batches, and fold in with a large metal spoon after each addition.

6 Transfer to an ungreased 25cm/ 10in tube tin (pan) and bake until just browned on top, about 1 hour.

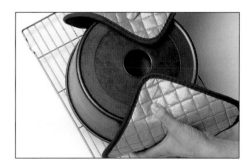

7 ▲ Turn the tin upside down on to a cake rack and leave to cool for 1 hour. If the cake does not turn out, run a knife around the edge to loosen it. Invert on a serving plate.

8 When cool, lay a star-shaped template on top of the cake, sift over icing sugar and remove template.

Marbled Ring Cake

SERVES 16

115g/4oz plain (semisweet) chocolate

350g/12oz/3 cups plain (all-purpose) flour

5ml/1 tsp baking powder

450g/1lb/2 cups butter, at room temperature

725g/1lb 10oz/3½ cups caster
   (superfine) sugar

15ml/1 tbsp vanilla extract

10 eggs, at room temperature

icing (confectioners') sugar, for dusting

1 ▲ Preheat the oven to 180°C/350°F/
Gas 4. Line a 25 × 10cm/10 × 4in ring
mould with baking parchment and
grease the paper. Dust with flour.

2 ▲ Melt the chocolate in the top of
a double boiler, or in a heatproof bowl
set over a pan of hot water. Stir
occasionally. Set aside.

3 In a bowl, sift together the flour
and baking powder. In another bowl,
cream the butter, sugar and vanilla
with an electric mixer until light and
fluffy. Add the eggs, two at a time,
then gradually incorporate the flour
mixture on low speed.

4 ▲ Spoon half of the mixture into
the prepared tin (pan).

5 ▲ Stir the chocolate into the
remaining mixture, then spoon into
the tin. With a metal spatula, swirl
the mixtures for a marbled effect.

6 Bake until a skewer inserted into
the centre comes out clean, about
1 hour 45 minutes. Cover with foil
halfway through baking. Leave to
stand for 15 minutes, then turn out
and transfer to a cooling rack. To
serve, dust with icing sugar.

Coffee-iced Ring

SERVES 16

275g/10oz/2¹/₂ cups plain (all-purpose) flour

15ml/1 tbsp baking powder

5ml/1 tsp salt

350g/12oz/1³/₄ cup caster (superfine) sugar

120ml/4fl oz/¹/₂ cup vegetable oil

7 eggs, at room temperature, separated

175ml/6fl oz/³/₄ cup cold water

10ml/2 tsp vanilla extract

10ml/2 tsp grated lemon rind

2.5ml/¹/₂ tsp cream of tartar

FOR THE ICING

165g/5¹/₂oz unsalted (sweet) butter

575g/1lb 4oz/5 cups icing (confectioners')
  sugar

20ml/4 tsp instant coffee dissolved in
  60ml/4 tbsp hot water

1 Preheat the oven to 170°C/325°F/
Gas 3.

2 ▼ Sift the flour, baking powder
and salt into a bowl. Stir in 225g/8oz
of the sugar. Make a well in the centre
and add the oil, egg yolks, water,
vanilla and lemon rind. Beat with a
whisk or metal spoon until smooth.

3 With an electric mixer, beat the
egg whites with the cream of tartar
until they hold soft peaks. Add the
remaining sugar and beat until the
mixture holds stiff peaks.

4 ▲ Pour the flour mixture over the
whites in three batches, folding well
after each addition.

5 Transfer the mixture to a 25 × 10cm/
10 × 4in ring mould and bake until
the top springs back when touched
lightly, about 1 hour.

6 ▲ When baked, remove from the
oven and immediately hang the cake
upside-down over the neck of a funnel
or a narrow bottle. Leave to cool. To
remove the cake, run a knife around
the inside to loosen, then turn the tin
over and tap the sides sharply. Invert
the cake on to a serving plate.

7 For the icing, beat together the
butter and icing sugar with an electric
mixer until smooth. Add the coffee
and beat until fluffy. With a metal
spatula, spread over the sides and top
of the cake.

Spice Cake with Cream Cheese Icing

SERVES 10–12

300ml/¹/₂ pint/1¹/₄ cups milk
30ml/2 tbsp golden (light corn) syrup
10ml/2 tsp vanilla extract
75g/3oz/¹/₂ cup walnuts, chopped
175g/6oz/³/₄ cup butter, at room temperature
300g/11oz/generous 1¹/₂ cups caster (superfine) sugar
1 egg, at room temperature
3 egg yolks, at room temperature
275g/10oz/2¹/₂ cups plain (all-purpose) flour
15ml/1 tbsp baking powder
5ml/1 tsp freshly grated nutmeg
5ml/1 tsp ground cinnamon
2.5ml/¹/₂ tsp ground cloves
1.5ml/¹/₄ tsp ground ginger
1.5ml/¹/₄ tsp ground allspice
FOR THE ICING
175g/6oz/³/₄ cup cream cheese
25g/1oz/2 tbsp unsalted (sweet) butter
200g/7oz/1³/₄ cups icing (confectioners') sugar
30ml/2 tbsp finely chopped stem ginger
30ml/2 tbsp syrup from stem ginger
stem ginger pieces, for decorating

1 Preheat the oven to 180°C/350°F/ Gas 4. Line three 20cm/8in cake tins (pans) with baking parchment and grease. In a bowl, combine the milk, syrup, vanilla and walnuts.

2 ▼ With an electric mixer, cream the butter and sugar until light and fluffy. Beat in the egg and egg yolks. Add the milk mixture and stir well.

3 Sift together the flour, baking powder and spices three times.

4 ▲ Add the flour mixture to the egg mixture in four batches, and fold in carefully after each addition.

5 Divide the cake mixture between the tins. Bake until the cakes spring back when touched lightly, about 25 minutes. Leave to stand for 5 minutes, then turn out and cool on a rack.

6 ▼ For the icing, combine all the ingredients and beat with an electric mixer. Spread the icing between the layers and over the top. Decorate with pieces of stem ginger.

Caramel Layer Cake

SERVES 8–10

275g/10oz/2¹/₂ cups plain (all-purpose) flour

7.5ml/1¹/₂ tsp baking powder

175g/6oz/³/₄ cup butter, at room temperature

165g/5¹/₂oz/generous ³/₄ cup caster (superfine) sugar

4 eggs, at room temperature, beaten

5ml/1 tsp vanilla extract

120ml/4fl oz/¹/₂ cup milk

whipped cream, for decorating

caramel threads, for decorating (optional, see below)

FOR THE ICING

300g/11oz/scant 1¹/₃ cups soft dark brown sugar

250ml/8fl oz/1 cup milk

25g/1oz/2 tbsp unsalted (sweet) butter

45–75ml/3–5 tbsp whipping cream

1 Preheat the oven to 180°C/350°F/Gas 4. Line two 20cm/8in cake tins (pans) with baking parchment; grease lightly.

2 ▲ Sift the flour and baking powder together three times. Set aside.

~ COOK'S TIP ~

To make caramel threads, combine 65g/2¹/₂oz/5 tbsp sugar and 50ml/2fl oz/¹/₄ cup water in a heavy pan. Boil until light brown. Dip the pan in cold water to halt cooking. Trail from a spoon on an oiled baking sheet.

3 With an electric mixer, cream the butter and caster sugar until light and fluffy.

4 ▲ Slowly mix in the beaten eggs. Add the vanilla. Fold in the flour mixture, alternating with the milk.

5 ▲ Divide the batter between the prepared tins and spread evenly, hollowing out the centres slightly.

6 Bake until the cakes pull away from the sides of the tin, about 30 minutes. Leave to stand for 5 minutes, then turn out and cool on a rack.

7 ▲ For the icing, combine the brown sugar and milk in a pan.

8 Bring to the boil, cover and cook for 3 minutes. Remove the lid and continue to boil, without stirring, until the mixture reaches 119°C/238°F (soft ball stage) on a sugar thermometer.

9 ▲ Immediately remove the pan from the heat and add the butter, but do not stir it in. Cool until lukewarm, then beat until the mixture is smooth and creamy.

10 Stir in enough cream to obtain a spreadable consistency. If necessary, chill to thicken more.

11 ▲ Spread a layer of icing on top of one cake. Sandwich with the second cake, then spread the top and sides with the rest of the icing and smooth the surface.

12 To decorate, pipe whipped cream rosettes around the edge. Place a mound of caramel threads, if using, in the centre before serving.

Lady Baltimore Cake

SERVES 8–10

275g/10oz/2½ cups plain (all-purpose) flour

12.5ml/2½ tsp baking powder

2.5ml/½ tsp salt

4 eggs

350g/12oz/1¾ cups caster (superfine) sugar

grated rind of 1 large orange

250ml/8fl oz/1 cup fresh orange juice

250ml/8fl oz/1 cup vegetable oil

18 pecan halves, for decorating

FOR THE FROSTING

2 egg whites

350g/12oz/1¾ cups caster sugar

75ml/5 tbsp cold water

1.5ml/¼ tsp cream of tartar

5ml/1 tsp vanilla extract

50g/2oz/⅓ cup pecan nuts, finely chopped

75g/3oz/⅔ cup raisins, chopped

3 dried figs, finely chopped

1 Preheat the oven to 180°C/350°F/Gas 4. Grease two 23cm/9in round cake tins (pans) and line with baking parchment. Grease the paper. In a bowl, sift together the flour, baking powder and salt. Set aside.

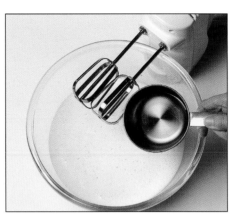

2 ▲ With an electric mixer, beat the eggs and sugar until thick and lemon-coloured. Beat in the orange rind and juice, then the oil.

3 On low speed, beat in the flour mixture in three batches. Divide the cake mixture between the tins.

4 ▲ Bake until a skewer inserted into the centre comes out clean, about 30 minutes. Leave to stand for 15 minutes, then run a knife around the inside of the cakes and transfer them to racks to cool completely.

5 ▲ For the icing, combine the egg whites, sugar, water and cream of tartar in the top of a double boiler, or in a heatproof bowl set over boiling water. With an electric mixer, beat until glossy and thick. Off the heat, add the vanilla extract and continue beating until thick. Fold in the pecan nuts, raisins and figs.

6 Spread a layer of icing on top of one cake. Sandwich with the second cake, then spread the top and sides with the rest of the icing. Arrange the pecan halves on top.

Carrot Cake

SERVES 12

450g/1lb carrots, peeled

175g/6oz/1½ cups plain (all-purpose) flour

10ml/2 tsp baking powder

2.5ml/½ tsp bicarbonate of soda
(baking soda)

5ml/1 tsp salt

10ml/2 tsp ground cinnamon

4 eggs

10ml/2 tsp vanilla extract

115g/4oz/½ cup soft dark brown sugar

50g/2oz/¼ cup caster (superfine) sugar

300ml/½ pint/1¼ cups sunflower oil

115g/4oz/1 cup finely chopped walnuts

75g/3oz/⅔ cup raisins

walnut halves, for decorating (optional)

FOR THE ICING

75g/3oz/6 tbsp unsalted (sweet) butter

350g/12oz/3 cups icing (confectioners')
sugar

50ml/2fl oz/¼ cup maple syrup

1 Preheat the oven to 180°C/350°F/
Gas 4. Line a 28 × 20cm/11 × 8in tin
(pan) with baking parchment; grease.

2 ▲ Grate the carrots and set aside.

3 Sift the flour, baking powder,
bicarbonate of soda, salt and
cinnamon into a bowl. Set aside.

4 With an electric mixer, beat the
eggs until blended. Add the vanilla,
sugars and oil; beat to incorporate. Add
the dry ingredients, in three batches,
folding in well after each addition.

5 ▲ Add the carrots, walnuts and
raisins, and fold in thoroughly.

6 Pour the mixture into the prepared
tin and bake until the cake springs
back when touched lightly, 40–45
minutes. Leave for 10 minutes, then
turn out and transfer to a rack.

7 ▼ For the icing, cream the butter
with half the icing sugar until soft.
Add the syrup, then beat in the
remaining sugar until blended.

8 Spread the icing over the top of the
cake. Using the tip of a metal spatula,
make decorative ridges in the icing.
Cut into squares. Decorate with
walnut halves, if you like.

Cranberry Upside-down Cake

SERVES 8

350–400g/12–14oz/3–3¹/₂ cups fresh cranberries
50g/2oz/¹/₄ cup butter
150g/5oz/³/₄ cup caster (superfine) sugar
FOR THE CAKE MIXTURE
65g/2¹/₂oz/9 tbsp plain (all-purpose) flour
5ml/1 tsp baking powder
3 eggs
115g/4oz/generous ¹/₂ cup sugar
grated rind of 1 orange
40g/1¹/₂oz/3 tbsp butter, melted

1 Preheat the oven to 180°C/350°F/ Gas 4. Place a baking sheet on the middle shelf of the oven.

2 Wash the cranberries and pat dry. Thickly smear the butter on the bottom and sides of a 23 × 5cm/ 9 × 2in round cake tin (pan). Add the sugar and swirl the tin to coat evenly.

3 ▲ Add the cranberries and spread in an even layer over the bottom of the tin.

4 For the cake mixture, sift the flour and baking powder twice. Set aside.

5 ▲ Combine the eggs, sugar and orange rind in a heatproof bowl set over a pan of hot but not boiling water. With an electric mixer, beat until the eggs leave a ribbon trail when the beaters are lifted.

6 Add the flour mixture in three batches, folding in well after each addition. Gently fold in the melted butter, then pour over the cranberries.

7 Bake for 40 minutes. Leave to cool for 5 minutes, then run a knife around the inside edge to loosen.

8 ▲ While the cake is still warm, invert a plate on top of the tin. Protecting your hands with oven gloves, hold the plate and tin firmly and turn them both over quickly. Lift off the tin carefully.

Pineapple Upside-down Cake

SERVES 8

115g/4oz/½ cup butter
200g/7oz/scant 1 cup soft dark brown sugar
450g/1lb canned pineapple slices, drained
4 eggs, separated
grated rind of 1 lemon
pinch of salt
115g/4oz/generous ½ cup caster (superfine) sugar
75g/3oz/⅔ cup plain (all-purpose) flour
5ml/1 tsp baking powder

1 Preheat the oven to 180°C/350°F/ Gas 4.

2 Melt the butter in a 25cm/10in ovenproof frying pan. Remove about 15ml/1 tbsp of the melted butter and set aside.

3 ▲ Add the brown sugar to the pan and stir until blended. Place the drained pineapple slices on top in one layer. Set aside.

4 In a bowl, whisk together the egg yolks, reserved butter and lemon rind until well blended. Set aside.

5 ▼ With an electric mixer, beat the egg whites with the salt until stiff. Fold in the caster sugar, 25g/1oz/ 2 tbsp at a time. Fold in the egg yolk mixture.

6 Sift the flour and baking powder together. Carefully fold into the egg mixture in three batches.

7 ▲ Pour the mixture over the pineapple and smooth level.

8 Bake until a skewer inserted into the centre comes out clean, about 30 minutes.

9 While still hot, place a serving plate on top of the pan, bottom-side up. Holding them tightly together with oven gloves, quickly flip over. Serve hot or cold.

~ VARIATION ~

For Apricot Upside-down Cake, replace the pineapple slices with 225g/8oz/1 cup ready-to-eat dried apricots. If they need softening, simmer them in about 120ml/4fl oz/½ cup orange juice until plump and soft. Drain the apricots and discard any remaining cooking liquid.

Lemon Coconut Layer Cake

SERVES 8–10

175g/6oz/1½ cups plain (all-purpose) flour
pinch of salt
7 eggs
350g/12oz/scant 1¾ cups caster (superfine) sugar
15ml/1 tbsp grated orange rind
grated rind of 2 lemons
juice of 1½ lemon
65g/2½oz/scant 1 cup desiccated (dry sweetened) coconut
15ml/1 tbsp cornflour (cornstarch)
120ml/4fl oz/½ cup water
40g/1½oz/3 tbsp butter
FOR THE ICING
75g/3oz/6 tbsp unsalted (sweet) butter
175g/6oz/1½ cups icing (confectioners') sugar
grated rind of 1½ lemons
30ml/2 tbsp lemon juice
200g/7oz/2½ cups desiccated (dry sweetened) coconut

1 Preheat the oven to 180°C/350°F/ Gas 4. Line three 20cm/8in cake tins (pans) with baking parchment and grease. In a bowl, sift together the flour and salt and set aside.

2 ▲ Place six of the eggs in a large heatproof bowl set over hot water. With an electric mixer, beat until frothy. Gradually beat in 225g/8oz/ generous 1 cup caster sugar until the mixture doubles in volume and leaves a ribbon trail when the beaters are lifted, about 10 minutes.

3 ▲ Remove the bowl from the hot water. Fold in the orange rind, half the grated lemon rind and 15ml/1 tbsp of the lemon juice until blended. Fold in the coconut.

4 Sift over the flour mixture in three batches, gently folding in thoroughly after each addition.

5 ▲ Divide the mixture between the prepared tins.

6 Bake until the cakes pull away from the sides of the tins, 20–25 minutes. Leave to stand for 3–5 minutes, then turn out to cool on a rack.

7 In a bowl, blend the cornflour with a little cold water to dissolve. Whisk in the remaining egg until just blended. Set aside.

8 ▲ In a pan, combine the remaining lemon rind and juice, the water, remaining sugar and butter.

9 Over medium heat, bring the mixture to the boil. Whisk in the eggs and cornflour mixture, and return to the boil. Whisk continuously until thick, about 5 minutes. Remove from the heat and pour into a bowl. Cover with clear film (plastic wrap); set aside.

10 ▲ For the frosting, cream the butter and icing sugar until smooth. Stir in the lemon rind and enough lemon juice to obtain a thick, spreadable consistency.

11 Sandwich the three cake layers with the lemon custard mixture. Spread the frosting over the top and sides. Cover the cake with the coconut, pressing it in gently.

Lemon Yogurt Ring

SERVES 12

225g/8oz/1 cup butter,
  at room temperature

300g/11oz/generous 1½ cups caster
  (superfine) sugar

4 eggs, at room temperature, separated

10ml/2 tsp grated lemon rind

85ml/3fl oz/generous ⅓ cup lemon juice

250ml/8fl oz/1 cup plain (natural) yogurt

275g/10oz/2½ cups plain
  (all-purpose) flour

10ml/2 tsp baking powder

5ml/1 tsp bicarbonate of soda
  (baking soda)

2.5ml/½ tsp salt

FOR THE GLAZE

115g/4oz/1 cup icing
  (confectioners') sugar

30ml/2 tbsp lemon juice

45–60ml/3–4 tbsp plain (natural) yogurt

1 Preheat oven to 180°C/350°F/Gas 4. Grease a 3 litre/5¼ pint/13¼ cup bundt or fluted tube tin (pan) and dust with flour.

2 With an electric mixer, cream the butter and caster sugar until light and fluffy. Add the egg yolks, one at a time, beating well after each addition.

3 ▲ Add the lemon rind, juice and yogurt, and stir to blend.

4 Sift together the flour, baking powder and bicarbonate of soda. In another bowl, beat the egg whites and salt until they hold stiff peaks.

5 ▲ Fold the dry ingredients into the butter mixture, then fold in a dollop of egg whites. Fold in the remaining whites until blended.

6 Pour into the tin and bake until a skewer inserted into the centre comes out clean, about 50 minutes. Leave to stand for 15 minutes, then turn out and cool on a rack.

7 For the glaze, sift the icing sugar into a bowl. Stir in the lemon juice and just enough yogurt to make a smooth glaze.

8 ▲ Set the cooled cake on the rack over a sheet of baking parchment or a baking sheet. Pour over the glaze and let it drip down the sides. Allow the glaze to set before serving.

Sour Cream Crumble Cake

SERVES 12–14

115g/4oz/½ cup butter, at room temperature

130g/4½oz/scant ¾ cup caster (superfine) sugar

3 eggs, at room temperature

215g/7½oz/scant 2 cups plain (all-purpose) flour

5ml/1 tsp bicarbonate of soda (baking soda)

5ml/1 tsp baking powder

250ml/8fl oz/1 cup sour cream

FOR THE TOPPING

225g/8oz/1 cup soft dark brown sugar

10ml/2 tsp ground cinnamon

115g/4oz/⅔ cup walnuts, finely chopped

50g/2oz/¼ cup cold butter, cut into pieces

1 Preheat the oven to 180°C/350°F/ Gas 4. Line the base of a 23cm/9in square cake tin (pan) with baking parchment and grease.

2 ▲ For the topping, place the brown sugar, cinnamon and walnuts in a bowl. Mix with your fingertips, then add the butter and continue working with your fingertips until the mixture resembles breadcrumbs.

3 To make the cake, cream the butter with an electric mixer until soft. Add the sugar and continue beating until the mixture is light and fluffy.

4 Add the eggs, one at a time, beating well after each addition.

5 In another bowl, sift the flour, bicarbonate of soda and baking powder together three times.

6 ▲ Fold the dry ingredients into the butter mixture in three batches, alternating with the sour cream. Fold until blended after each addition.

7 ▲ Pour half the batter into the prepared tin and sprinkle over half the walnut crumb topping mixture.

8 Pour the remaining batter on top and sprinkle over the remaining walnut crumb mixture.

9 Bake until browned, 60–70 minutes. Leave to stand for 5 minutes, then turn out and cool on a rack.

Plum Crumble Cake

SERVES 8–10

150g/5oz/10 tbsp butter or margarine, at room temperature
150g/5oz/³⁄₄ cup caster (superfine) sugar
4 eggs, at room temperature
7.5ml/1¹⁄₂ tsp vanilla extract
150g/5oz/1¹⁄₄ cups plain flour
5ml/1 tsp baking powder
675g/1¹⁄₂lb red plums, halved and stoned (pitted)
FOR THE TOPPING
115g/4oz/1 cup plain (all-purpose) flour
130g/4¹⁄₂oz/generous ¹⁄₂ cup soft light brown sugar
7.5ml/1¹⁄₂ tsp ground cinnamon
75g/3oz/6 tbsp butter, cut in pieces

1 Preheat the oven to 180°C/350°F/ Gas 4.

2 For the topping, combine the flour, light brown sugar and cinnamon in a bowl. Add the butter and work the mixture with your fingertips until it resembles coarse breadcrumbs. Set aside.

3 ▲ Line a 25 × 5cm/10 × 2in tin (pan) with baking parchment and grease.

4 Cream the butter and sugar until light and fluffy.

5 ▲ Beat in the eggs, one at a time. Stir in the vanilla.

6 In a bowl, sift together the flour and baking powder, then fold into the butter mixture in three batches.

7 ▲ Pour the mixture into the tin. Arrange the plums on top.

8 ▲ Sprinkle the topping over the plums in an even layer.

9 Bake until a skewer inserted into the centre comes out clean, about 45 minutes. Leave to cool in the tin.

10 To serve, run a knife around the inside edge and invert on to a plate. Invert again on to a serving plate so that the topping is right-side up.

~ VARIATION ~

This cake can also be made with the same quantity of apricots, peeled, if preferred, or stoned cherries, or use a mixture of fruit, such as red or yellow plums, greengages and apricots.

Peach Torte

SERVES 8

115g/4oz/1 cup plain (all-purpose) flour
5ml/1 tsp baking powder
pinch of salt
115g/4oz/¹/₂ cup unsalted (sweet) butter, at room temperature
175g/6oz/scant 1 cup caster (superfine) sugar
2 eggs, at room temperature
6–7 peaches
sugar and lemon juice, for sprinkling
whipped cream, for serving (optional)

1 Preheat the oven to 180°C/350°F/ Gas 4. Grease a 25cm/10in springform cake tin (pan).

2 ▲ Sift together the flour, baking powder and salt. Set aside.

3 With an electric mixer, cream the butter and sugar until light and fluffy. Beat in the eggs, then fold in the dry ingredients until blended.

4 ▲ Spoon the mixture into the tin and smooth it to make an even layer over the bottom.

5 ▼ To skin the peaches, drop several at a time into a pan of gently boiling water. Boil for 10 seconds, then remove with a slotted spoon. Peel off the skin with the aid of a sharp knife. Cut the peaches in half and discard the stones (pits).

6 ▲ Arrange the peach halves on top of the mixture. Sprinkle lightly with sugar and lemon juice.

7 Bake until golden brown and set, 50–60 minutes. Serve warm, with whipped cream, if you like.

Apple Ring Cake

SERVES 12

7 eating apples, such as Cox's or Granny Smith
350ml/12fl oz/1½ cups vegetable oil
450g/1lb/2¼ cups caster (superfine) sugar
3 eggs
425g/15oz/3½ cups plain (all-purpose) flour
5ml/1 tsp salt
5ml/1 tsp bicarbonate of soda (baking soda)
5ml/1 tsp ground cinnamon
5ml/1 tsp vanilla extract
115g/4oz/1 cup chopped walnuts
175g/6oz/generous 1 cup raisins
icing (confectioners') sugar, for dusting

1 Preheat the oven to 180°C/350°F/ Gas 4. Grease a 23cm/9in ring mould.

2 ▲ Quarter, peel, core and slice the apples into a bowl. Set aside.

3 With an electric mixer, beat the oil and sugar together until blended. Add the eggs and continue beating until the mixture is creamy.

4 Sift together the flour, salt, bicarbonate of soda and cinnamon.

5 ▼ Fold the flour mixture into the egg mixture with the vanilla. Stir in the apples, walnuts and raisins.

6 Pour into the tin (pan) and bake until the cake springs back when touched lightly, about 1¼ hours. Leave to stand for 15 minutes, then turn out and transfer to a cooling rack. Dust with a layer of icing sugar before serving.

Orange Cake

SERVES 6

175g/6oz/1½ cups plain (all-purpose) flour
pinch of salt
7.5ml/1½ tsp baking powder
115g/4oz/½ cup butter or margarine
115g/4oz/generous ½ cup caster (superfine) sugar
grated rind of 1 large orange
2 eggs, at room temperature
30ml/2 tbsp milk
FOR THE SYRUP AND DECORATION
115g/4oz/generous ½ cup caster (superfine) sugar
250ml/8fl oz/1 cup fresh orange juice, strained
3 orange slices, for decorating

1 Preheat the oven to 180°C/350°F/ Gas 4. Line a 20cm/8in cake tin (pan) with baking parchment and grease the paper.

2 ▲ Sift the flour, salt and baking powder on to baking parchment.

3 With an electric mixer, cream the butter or margarine until soft. Add the sugar and orange rind, and beat until light and fluffy. Beat in the eggs, one at a time. Fold in the flour in three batches, then add the milk.

4 Spoon into the tin and bake until the cake pulls away from the sides, about 30 minutes. Remove from the oven but leave in the tin.

5 Meanwhile, for the syrup, dissolve the sugar in the orange juice over a low heat. Add the orange slices and simmer for 10 minutes. Remove and drain. Leave the syrup to cool.

6 ▲ Prick the cake all over with a fine skewer. Pour the syrup over the hot cake. It may seem at first that there is too much syrup for the cake to absorb, but it will soak it all up. Turn out when completely cooled and decorate with small triangles of the orange slices arranged on top.

Apple Ring Cake (top), Orange Cake

Orange and Walnut Roll

SERVES 8

4 eggs, separated

115g/4oz/generous ½ cup caster
   (superfine) sugar

115g/4oz/1 cup very finely chopped walnuts

pinch of cream of tartar

pinch of salt

icing (confectioners') sugar, for dusting

FOR THE FILLING

300ml/½ pint/1¼ cups whipping cream

15ml/1 tbsp caster (superfine) sugar

grated rind of 1 orange

15ml/1 tbsp orange liqueur, such as
   Grand Marnier

1 Preheat the oven to 180°C/350°F/
Gas 4. Line a 30 × 24cm/12 × 9½in
Swiss roll tin (jelly roll pan) with
baking parchment and grease the paper.

2 With an electric mixer, beat the
egg yolks and sugar until thick.

3 ▲ Stir in the walnuts.

4 In another bowl, beat the egg
whites with the cream of tartar and
salt until they hold stiff peaks. Fold
gently but thoroughly into the
walnut mixture.

5 Pour the mixture into the prepared
tin and spread level with a spatula.
Bake for 15 minutes.

6 Run a knife along the inside edge
to loosen, then invert the cake on to
a sheet of baking parchment dusted
with icing sugar.

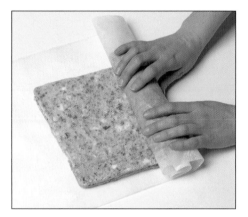

7 ▲ Peel off the baking parchment.
Roll up the cake while it is still warm
with the help of the sugared paper.
Set aside to cool.

8 For the filling, whip the cream
until it holds soft peaks. Stir together
the caster sugar and orange rind, then
fold into the whipped cream. Add
the liqueur.

9 ▲ Gently unroll the cake.
Spread the inside with a layer of
orange whipped cream, then re-roll.
Keep chilled until ready to serve.
Dust the top with icing sugar just
before serving.

Chocolate Roll

SERVES 10

225g/8oz plain (semisweet) chocolate

45ml/3 tbsp water

30ml/2 tbsp rum, brandy or strong coffee

7 eggs, separated

175g/6oz/scant 1 cup caster
(superfine) sugar

pinch of salt

350ml/12fl oz/1½ cups whipping cream

icing (confectioners') sugar, for dusting

1 Preheat the oven to 180°C/350°F/ Gas 4. Line a 38 × 33cm/15 × 13in Swiss roll tin (jelly roll pan) with baking parchment and grease the paper.

2 ▲ Combine the chocolate, water and rum or other flavouring in the top of a double boiler, or in a heatproof bowl set over hot water. Heat until melted. Set aside.

3 With an electric mixer, beat the egg yolks and sugar until thick.

4 ▲ Stir in the melted chocolate.

5 In another bowl, beat the egg whites and salt until they hold stiff peaks. Fold a large dollop of the egg whites into the yolk mixture to lighten it, then carefully fold in the rest of the whites.

6 ▼ Pour the mixture into the pan; smooth evenly with a metal spatula.

7 Bake for 15 minutes. Remove from the oven, cover with baking parchment and a damp dish towel. Leave to stand for 1–2 hours.

8 With an electric mixer, whip the cream until stiff. Set aside.

9 Run a knife along the inside edge to loosen, then invert the cake on to a sheet of baking parchment that has been dusted with icing sugar.

10 Peel off the baking parchment. Spread with an even layer of whipped cream, then roll up the cake with the help of the sugared paper.

11 Chill for several hours. Before serving, dust with an even layer of icing sugar.

Chocolate Frosted Layer Cake

SERVES 8

225g/8oz/1 cup butter or margarine, at room temperature

300g/11oz/generous 1½ cups caster (superfine) sugar

4 eggs, at room temperature, separated

10ml/2 tsp vanilla extract

385g/13½oz/3⅓ cups plain (all-purpose) flour

10ml/2 tsp baking powder

pinch of salt

250ml/8fl oz/1 cup milk

FOR THE ICING

150g/5oz plain (semisweet) chocolate

120ml/4fl oz/½ cup sour cream

pinch of salt

1 Preheat the oven to 180°C/350°F/Gas 4. Line two 20cm/8in round cake tins (pans) with baking parchment and grease. Dust with flour and shake to distribute. Tap to dislodge excess flour.

2 With an electric mixer, cream the butter or margarine until soft. Gradually add the sugar and continue beating until light and fluffy.

3 ▲ Lightly beat the egg yolks, then mix into the creamed butter and sugar with the vanilla.

4 Sift the flour with the baking powder three times. Set aside.

5 In another bowl, beat the egg whites with the salt until they hold stiff peaks. Set aside.

6 ▲ Gently fold the dry ingredients into the butter mixture in three batches, alternating with the milk.

7 Add a large dollop of the whites and fold in to lighten the mixture. Carefully fold in the remaining whites until just blended.

8 Divide the batter between the tins and bake until the cakes pull away from the sides of the tins, about 30 minutes. Leave to stand for 5 minutes. Turn out and cool on a rack.

9 ▲ For the icing, melt the chocolate in the top of a double boiler or a bowl set over hot water. When cool, stir in the sour cream and salt.

10 Sandwich the layers with icing, then spread on the top and side.

Devil's Food Cake with Orange Icing

SERVES 8–10

50g/2oz/¹/₂ cup unsweetened cocoa powder

175ml/6fl oz/³/₄ cup boiling water

175g/6oz/³/₄ cup butter, at room temperature

350g/12oz/1¹/₂ cups soft dark brown sugar

3 eggs, at room temperature

275g/10oz/2¹/₂ cups plain (all-purpose) flour

7.5ml/1¹/₂ tsp bicarbonate of soda
  (baking soda)

1.5ml/¹/₄ tsp baking powder

120ml/4fl oz/¹/₂ cup sour cream

orange rind strips, for decoration

FOR THE ICING

300g/11oz/generous 1¹/₂ cups caster
  (superfine) sugar

2 egg whites

60ml/4 tbsp frozen orange juice concentrate

15ml/1 tbsp lemon juice

grated rind of 1 orange

1 Preheat the oven to 180°C/350°F/
Gas 4. Line two 23cm/9in cake tins
(pans) with baking parchment and
grease. In a bowl, mix the cocoa
and water until smooth. Set aside.

2 With an electric mixer, cream the
butter and sugar until light and fluffy.
Add the eggs, one at a time, beating
well after each addition.

3 ▲ When the cocoa mixture is
lukewarm, add to the butter mixture.

4 ▼ Sift together the flour, soda and
baking powder twice. Fold into the
cocoa mixture in three batches,
alternating with the sour cream.

5 Pour into the tins and bake until
the cakes pull away from the sides
of the tins, 30–35 minutes. Leave for
15 minutes. Turn out on to a rack.

6 Thinly slice the orange rind strips.
Blanch in boiling water for 1 minute.

7 ▲ For the icing, place all the
ingredients in the top of a double
boiler or in a bowl set over hot water.
With an electric mixer, beat until the
mixture holds soft peaks. Continue
beating off the heat until thick
enough to spread.

8 Sandwich the cake layers with
icing, then spread over the top
and side. Arrange the blanched
orange rind strips on top of the cake.

Best-ever Chocolate Sandwich

Serves 12–14

115g/4oz/¹/₂ cup unsalted (sweet) butter
115g/4oz/1 cup plain (all-purpose) flour
50g/2oz/¹/₂ cup unsweetened cocoa powder
5ml/1 tsp baking powder
pinch of salt
6 eggs
225g/8oz/generous 1 cup caster (superfine) sugar
10ml/2 tsp vanilla extract
For the icing
225g/8oz plain (semisweet) chocolate,
75g/3oz/6 tbsp unsalted butter
3 eggs, separated
250ml/8fl oz/1 cup whipping cream
45ml/3 tbsp caster sugar

1 Preheat the oven to 180°C/350°F/ Gas 4. Line three 20 × 3cm/8 × 1¹/₂in round tins (pans) with baking parchment and grease.

2 ▲ Dust evenly with flour and spread with a brush. Set aside.

~ **VARIATION** ~

For a simpler icing, combine 250ml/ 8fl oz/1 cup whipping cream with 225g/8oz finely chopped plain chocolate in a pan. Stir over a low heat until the chocolate has melted. Cool and whisk to spreading consistency.

3 ▲ Melt the butter over a low heat. With a spoon, skim off any foam that rises to the surface. Set aside.

4 ▲ Sift the flour, cocoa, baking powder and salt together three times and set aside.

5 Place the eggs and sugar in a large heatproof bowl set over a pan of hot water. With an electric mixer, beat until the mixture doubles in volume and is thick enough to leave a ribbon trail when the beaters are lifted, about 10 minutes. Add the vanilla.

6 ▲ Sift over the dry ingredients in three batches, folding in carefully after each addition. Fold in the butter.

7 Divide the mixture between the tins and bake until the cakes pull away from the sides of the tin, about 25 minutes. Transfer to a rack.

8 For the icing, chop the chocolate and melt in the top of a double boiler, or in a heatproof bowl set over hot water.

9 ▲ Off the heat, stir in the butter and egg yolks. Return to a low heat and stir until thick. Remove from the heat and set aside.

10 Whip the cream until firm; set aside. In another bowl, beat the egg whites until stiff. Add the sugar and beat until glossy.

11 Fold the cream into the chocolate mixture, then carefully fold in the egg whites. Chill for 20 minutes to thicken the icing.

12 ▲ Sandwich the cake layers with icing, stacking them carefully. Spread the remaining icing evenly over the top and sides of the cake.

Rich Chocolate Nut Cake

SERVES 10

225g/8oz/1 cup butter

225g/8oz plain (semisweet) chocolate

115g/4oz/1 cup unsweetened cocoa powder

350g/12oz/1¾ cups caster (superfine) sugar

6 eggs

85ml/3fl oz/generous ⅓ cup brandy or cognac

225g/8oz/2 cups finely chopped hazelnuts

FOR THE GLAZE

50g/2oz/¼ cup butter

150g/5oz dark (bittersweet) chocolate

30ml/2 tbsp milk

5ml/1 tsp vanilla essence extract

1 Preheat the oven to 180°C/350°F/ Gas 4. Line a 23 × 5cm/9 × 2in round tin (pan) with baking parchment; grease.

2 Melt the butter and chocolate together in the top of a double boiler, or in a heatproof bowl set over hot water. Set aside to cool.

3 ▼ Sift the cocoa into a bowl. Add the sugar and eggs, and stir until just combined. Pour in the melted chocolate mixture and brandy.

4 Fold in three-quarters of the nuts, then pour the mixture into the prepared tin.

5 ▲ Set the tin inside a roasting pan containing 2.5cm/1in of hot water. Bake until the cake is firm to the touch, about 45 minutes. Leave to stand for 15 minutes, then turn out and transfer to a cooling rack.

6 Wrap the cake in baking parchment and chill for 6 hours.

7 For the glaze, combine the butter, chocolate, milk and vanilla in the top of a double boiler or in a heatproof bowl set over hot water, until melted.

8 Place a piece of baking parchment under the cake, then drizzle spoonfuls of glaze along the edge to drip down and coat the sides. Pour the remaining glaze on top of the cake.

9 ▲ Cover the sides of the cake with the remaining nuts, gently pressing them on with the palm of your hand.

Chocolate Layer Cake

SERVES 8–10

115g/4oz plain (semisweet) chocolate

175g/6oz/³/₄ cup butter

450g/1lb/2¹/₄ cups caster (superfine) sugar

3 eggs

5ml/1 tsp vanilla extract

175g/6oz/1¹/₂ cups plain (all-purpose) flour

5ml/1 tsp baking powder

115g/4oz/1 cup chopped walnuts

FOR THE TOPPING

350ml/12fl oz/1¹/₂ cups whipping cream

225g/8oz plain chocolate

15ml/1 tbsp vegetable oil

1 Preheat the oven to 180°C/350°F/ Gas 4. Line two 20cm/8in cake tins (pans), at least 4.5cm/1¹/₂in deep, with baking parchment and grease.

2 Melt the chocolate and butter together in the top of a double boiler, or in a heatproof bowl set over a pan of hot water.

3 ▲ Transfer to a mixing bowl and stir in the sugar. Add the eggs and vanilla, and mix until well blended.

4 ▲ Sift over the flour and baking powder. Stir in the walnuts.

5 Divide the mixture between the prepared tins and spread level.

6 Bake until a skewer inserted into the centre comes out clean, about 30 minutes. Leave for 10 minutes, then turn out and transfer to a rack.

7 When the cakes are cool, whip the cream until firm. With a long serrated knife, carefully slice each cake in half horizontally.

8 Sandwich the layers with some of the whipped cream and spread the remainder over the top and sides of the cake. Chill until needed.

9 ▼ For the chocolate curls, melt the chocolate and oil in the top of a double boiler or a bowl set over hot water. Transfer to a non-porous surface. Spread to a 1cm/¹/₂in thick rectangle. Just before the chocolate sets, hold the blade of a straight knife at an angle to the chocolate and scrape across the surface to make curls. Place on top of the cake.

~ **VARIATION** ~

To make Chocolate Ice Cream Layer Cake, sandwich the cake layers with softened vanilla ice cream. Freeze before serving.

Sachertorte

SERVES 8–10

115g/4oz plain (semisweet) chocolate
75g/3oz/6 tbsp unsalted (sweet) butter, at room temperature
50g/2oz/¹/4 cup caster (superfine) sugar
4 eggs, separated
1 extra egg white
1.5ml/¹/4 tsp salt
65g/2¹/2oz/9 tbsp plain (all-purpose) flour, sifted
FOR THE TOPPING
75ml/5 tbsp apricot jam
250ml/8fl oz/1 cup plus 15ml/1 tbsp water
15g/¹/2oz/1 tbsp unsalted butter
175g/6oz plain chocolate
75g/3oz/scant ¹/2 cup caster sugar
ready-made chocolate decorating icing (optional)

1 Preheat the oven to 160°C/325°F/ Gas 3. Line a 23 × 5cm/9 × 2in cake tin (pan) with greaseproof paper and grease.

2 ▲ Melt the chocolate in the top of a double boiler, or in a heatproof bowl set over hot water. Set aside.

3 With an electric mixer, cream the butter and sugar until light and fluffy. Stir in the chocolate.

4 ▲ Beat in the yolks, one at a time.

5 In another bowl, beat the egg whites with the salt until stiff.

6 ▲ Fold a dollop of whites into the chocolate mixture to lighten it. Fold in the remaining whites in three batches, alternating with the sifted flour.

7 ▲ Pour into the tin and bake until a skewer comes out clean, about 45 minutes. Turn out on to a rack.

8 ▲ Meanwhile, melt the jam with 15ml/1 tbsp of the water over low heat, then strain for a smooth consistency.

9 For the frosting, melt the butter and chocolate in the top of a double boiler or a bowl set over hot water.

10 ▲ In a heavy pan, dissolve the sugar in the remaining water over low heat. Raise the heat and boil until it reaches 107°C/225°F (thread stage) on a sugar thermometer. Immediately plunge the bottom of the pan into cold water for 1 minute. Pour into the chocolate mixture and stir to blend. Leave to cool for a few minutes.

11 To assemble, brush the warm jam over the cake. Starting in the centre, pour over the frosting and work outward in a circular movement. Tilt the rack to spread; use a palette knife to smooth the side of the cake. Leave to set overnight. If you like, decorate with chocolate icing.

Raspberry and Hazelnut Meringue Cake

SERVES 8

150g/5oz/1¼ cups hazelnuts

4 egg whites

pinch of salt

200g/7oz/1 cup caster (superfine) sugar

2.5ml/½ tsp vanilla extract

FOR THE FILLING

300ml/½ pint/1¼ cups whipping cream

675g/1½lb raspberries

1 Preheat the oven to 180°C/350°F/ Gas 4. Line the base of two 20cm/8in cake tins (pans) with baking parchment and grease.

2 Spread the hazelnuts on a baking sheet and bake until lightly toasted, about 8 minutes. Cool slightly.

3 ▲ Rub the hazelnuts vigorously in a clean dishtowel to remove most of the skins.

4 Grind the nuts in a food processor, blender, or coffee grinder until they are the consistency of coarse sand.

5 Reduce oven to 150°C/300°F/Gas 2.

6 With an electric mixer, beat the egg whites and salt until they hold stiff peaks. Beat in 25g/1oz/2 tbsp of the sugar, then fold in the remaining sugar, a few tablespoons at a time, with a rubber scraper. Fold in the vanilla and the hazelnuts.

7 ▲ Divide the batter between the prepared tins and spread level.

8 Bake for 1¼ hours. If the meringues brown too quickly, protect with a sheet of foil. Leave to stand for 5 minutes, then carefully run a knife around the inside edge of the tins to loosen. Turn out on to a rack to cool.

9 For the filling, whip the cream until just firm.

10 ▲ Spread half the cream in an even layer on one meringue round and top with half the raspberries.

11 Top with the other meringue round. Spread the remaining cream on top and arrange the remaining raspberries over the cream. Chill for 1 hour for easy cutting.

Nut and Apple Gâteau

SERVES 8

115g/4oz/²/₃ cup pecan nuts or walnuts

50g/2oz/¹/₂ cup plain (all-purpose) flour

10ml/2 tsp baking powder

1.5ml/¹/₄ tsp salt

2 large cooking apples

3 eggs

225g/8oz/generous 1 cup caster
   (superfine) sugar

5ml/1 tsp vanilla extract

175ml/6fl oz/³/₄ cup whipping cream

1 Preheat the oven to 160°C/325°F/ Gas 3. Line two 23cm/9in cake tins (pans) with baking parchment and grease the paper. Spread the nuts on a baking sheet and bake for 10 minutes.

2 Finely chop the nuts. Reserve 20g/ ³/₄oz/1¹/₂ tbsp and place the rest in a mixing bowl. Sift over the flour, baking powder and salt, and stir.

3 ▲ Quarter, core and peel the apples. Cut into 3mm/¹/₈in dice, then stir into the nut-flour mixture.

4 ▲ With an electric mixer, beat the eggs until frothy. Gradually add the sugar and vanilla, and beat until a ribbon forms, about 8 minutes. Gently fold in the flour mixture.

5 Pour into the tins and level the tops. Bake until a skewer inserted into the centre comes out clean, about 35 minutes. Leave to stand for 10 minutes.

6 ▲ To loosen, run a knife around the inside edge of each layer. Cool.

7 ▲ Whip the cream until firm. Spread half over the cake. Top with the second cake. Pipe whipped cream rosettes on top and sprinkle over the reserved nuts before serving.

Almond Cake

SERVES 4–6

225g/8oz/1¹/₃ cups blanched whole almonds, plus more for decorating
25g/1oz/2 tbsp butter
75g/3oz/6 tbsp icing (confectioners') sugar
3 eggs
2.5ml/¹/₂ tsp almond extract
25g/1oz/¹/₄ cup plain (all-purpose) flour
3 egg whites
15ml/1 tbsp caster (superfine) sugar

1 ▲ Preheat the oven to 160°C/325°F/ Gas 3. Line a 23cm/9in round cake tin (pan) with baking parchment; grease.

2 ▲ Spread the almonds in a baking tray and toast for 10 minutes. Cool, then coarsely chop 185g/6¹/₂oz/generous 1 cup.

3 Melt the butter and set aside. Increase oven temperature to 200°C/400°F/Gas 6.

4 Grind the chopped almonds with half the icing sugar in a food processor, blender or grinder. Transfer to a mixing bowl.

5 ▲ Add the whole eggs and remaining icing sugar. With an electric mixer, beat until the mixture forms a ribbon when the beaters are lifted. Mix in the butter and almond essence. Sift over the flour and fold in gently.

6 With an electric mixer, beat the egg whites until they hold soft peaks. Add the caster sugar and beat until stiff and glossy.

7 ▲ Fold the whites into the almond mixture in four batches.

8 Spoon the mixture into the prepared tin and bake in the centre of the oven until golden brown, about 15–20 minutes. Decorate the top with the remaining toasted whole almonds. Serve warm.

Walnut Coffee Gâteau

SERVES 8–10

150g/5oz/1¼ cups walnuts
165g/5½oz/generous ¾ cup caster (superfine) sugar
5 eggs, separated
50g/2oz/1 cup dry breadcrumbs
15ml/1 tbsp unsweetened cocoa powder
15ml/1 tbsp instant coffee
30ml/2 tbsp rum or lemon juice
pinch of salt
90ml/6 tbsp redcurrant jelly
chopped walnuts, for decorating
FOR THE ICING
225g/8oz plain (semisweet) chocolate
750ml/1¼ pints/3 cups whipping cream

1 ▲ For the icing, combine the chocolate and cream in the top of a double boiler, or in a heatproof bowl set over simmering water. Stir until the chocolate melts. Leave to cool, then cover and chill overnight or until the mixture is firm.

2 Preheat the oven to 180°C/350°F/Gas 4. Line a 23 × 5cm/9 × 2in cake tin (pan) with baking parchment and grease.

3 ▲ Grind the nuts with 40g/1½oz/ 3 tbsp of the sugar in a food processor, blender, or coffee grinder.

4 With an electric mixer, beat the egg yolks and remaining sugar until thick and lemon-coloured.

5 ▲ Fold in the walnuts. Stir in the breadcrumbs, cocoa, coffee and rum or lemon juice.

6 ▲ In another bowl, beat the egg whites with the salt until they hold stiff peaks. Fold carefully into the walnut mixture with a rubber scraper.

7 Pour the meringue batter into the prepared tin and bake until the top of the cake springs back when touched lightly, about 45 minutes. Let the cake stand for 5 minutes, then turn out and cool on a rack.

8 ▲ When cool, slice the cake in half horizontally.

9 With an electric mixer, beat the chocolate icing mixture on low speed until it becomes lighter, about 30 seconds. Do not overbeat or it may become grainy.

10 ▲ Warm the jelly in a pan until melted, then brush over the cut cake layer. Spread with some of the chocolate icing, then sandwich with the remaining cake layer. Brush the top of the cake with jelly, then cover the side and top with the remaining chocolate icing. Make a starburst pattern by pressing gently with a table knife in lines radiating from the centre. Arrange the chopped walnuts around the edge.

Light Fruit Cake

MAKES 2 LOAVES

225g/8oz/1 cup prunes
225g/8oz/1½ cups dates
225g/8oz/1 cup currants
225g/8oz/1⅓ cups sultanas (golden raisins)
250ml/8fl oz/1 cup dry white wine
250ml/8fl oz/1 cup rum
350g/12oz/3 cups plain (all-purpose) flour
10ml/2 tsp baking powder
5ml/1 tsp ground cinnamon
2.5ml/½ tsp freshly grated nutmeg
225g/8oz/1 cup butter, at room temperature
225g/8oz/generous 1 cup caster (superfine) sugar
4 eggs, at room temperature, lightly beaten
5ml/1 tsp vanilla extract

1 Pit the prunes and dates and chop finely. Place in a bowl with the currants and sultanas.

2 ▲ Stir in the wine and rum and leave to stand, covered, for 48 hours. Stir occasionally.

3 Preheat the oven to 150°C/300°F/ Gas 2 with a tray of hot water in the bottom. Line two 23 × 13cm/9 × 5in tins (pans) with baking parchment; grease.

4 Sift together the flour, baking powder, cinnamon, and nutmeg.

5 ▲ With an electric mixer, cream the butter and sugar together until light and fluffy.

6 Gradually add the eggs and vanilla. Fold in the flour mixture in three batches. Fold in the dried fruit mixture and its soaking liquid.

7 ▲ Divide the mixture between the tins and bake until a skewer inserted into the centre comes out clean, about 1½ hours.

8 Leave the cake to stand for 20 minutes, then turn out and transfer to a cooling rack. Wrap in foil and store in an airtight container. If possible, leave for at least 1 week before serving to allow the flavours to mellow.

Rich Fruit Cake

SERVES 12

150g/5oz/²⁄₃ cup currants

175g/6oz/generous 1 cup raisins

50g/2oz/¹⁄₃ cup sultanas (golden raisins)

50g/2oz/¹⁄₄ cup glacé (candied)
  cherries, halved

45ml/3 tbsp sweet sherry

175g/6oz/³⁄₄ cup butter

200g/7oz/scant 1 cup soft dark
  brown sugar

2 eggs, at room temperature

200g/7oz/1³⁄₄ cups plain (all-purpose) flour

10ml/2 tsp baking powder

10ml/2 tsp each ground ginger, allspice,
  and cinnamon

15ml/1 tbsp golden (light corn) syrup

15ml/1 tbsp milk

50g/2oz/¹⁄₃ cup cut mixed (candied) peel

115g/4oz/1 cup chopped walnuts

FOR THE DECORATION

225g/8oz/generous 1 cup caster
  (superfine) sugar

120ml/4fl oz/¹⁄₂ cup water

1 lemon, thinly sliced

¹⁄₂ orange, thinly sliced

120ml/4fl oz/¹⁄₂ cup orange marmalade

glacé cherries

1 One day before preparing, combine the currants, raisins, sultanas and cherries in a bowl. Stir in the sherry. Cover and leave overnight to soak.

2 Preheat the oven to 150°C/300°F/ Gas 2. Line a 23 × 7.5cm/9 × 3in springform cake tin (pan) with baking parchment and grease. Place a tray of hot water on the bottom of the oven.

3 With an electric mixer, cream the butter and sugar until light and fluffy. Beat in the eggs, one at a time.

4 ▲ Sift the flour, baking powder and spices together three times. Fold into the butter mixture in three batches. Fold in the syrup, milk, dried fruit and liquid, mixed peel and nuts.

5 ▲ Spoon into the tin, spreading out so there is a slight depression in the centre of the mixture.

6 Bake until a skewer inserted into the centre comes out clean, 2¹⁄₂–3 hours. Cover with foil when the top is golden to prevent over-browning. Cool in the tin on a rack.

7 ▲ For the decoration, combine the sugar and water in a pan and bring to the boil. Add the lemon and orange slices and cook until crystallized, about 20 minutes. Work in batches, if necessary. Remove the fruit with a slotted spoon. Pour the remaining syrup over the cake and cool. Melt the marmalade over low heat, then brush over the top of the cake. Decorate with the crystallized citrus slices and cherries.

Whiskey Cake

MAKES 1 LOAF

175g/6oz/1¹/₂ cups chopped walnuts
75g/3oz/²/₃ cup raisins, chopped
75g/3oz/²/₃ cup currants
115g/4oz/1 cup plain (all-purpose) flour
5ml/1 tsp baking powder
1.5ml/¹/₄ tsp salt
115g/4oz/¹/₂ cup butter
225g/8oz/1 cup caster (superfine) sugar
3 eggs, at room temperature, separated
5ml/1 tsp freshly grated nutmeg
2.5ml/¹/₂ tsp ground cinnamon
85ml/3fl oz/generous ¹/₃ cup Irish whiskey
icing (confectioners') sugar, for dusting

1 ▼ Preheat the oven to 160°C/ 325°F/Gas 3. Line a 23 × 13cm/9 × 5in loaf tin (pan) with baking parchment. Grease the paper and sides of the pan.

2 ▲ Place the walnuts, raisins, and currants in a bowl. Sprinkle over 15g/ ¹/₂oz/2 tbsp of the flour, mix and set aside. Sift together the remaining flour, baking powder and salt.

3 ▲ Cream the butter and sugar until light and fluffy. Beat in the egg yolks.

4 Mix the nutmeg, cinnamon and whiskey. Fold into the butter mixture, alternating with the flour mixture.

5 ▲ In another bowl, beat the egg whites until stiff. Fold into the whiskey mixture until just blended. Fold in the walnut mixture.

6 Bake until a skewer inserted into the centre comes out clean, about 1 hour. Cool in the pan. Dust with icing sugar over a template.

Gingerbread

SERVES 8–10

15ml/1 tbsp vinegar
175ml/6fl oz/³/4 cup milk
175g/6oz/1¹/2 cups plain (all-purpose) flour
10ml/2 tsp baking powder
1.5ml/¹/4 tsp bicarbonate of soda (baking soda)
2.5ml/¹/2 tsp salt
10ml/2 tsp ground ginger
5ml/1 tsp ground cinnamon
1.5ml/¹/4 tsp ground cloves
115g/4oz/¹/2 cup butter, at room temperature
115g/4oz/generous ¹/2 cup caster (superfine) sugar
1 egg, at room temperature
175ml/6fl oz/³/4 cup black treacle (molasses)
whipped cream, for serving
chopped stem ginger, for decorating

1 ▲ Preheat the oven to 180°C/350°F/ Gas 4. Line an 20cm/8in square cake tin (pan) with baking parchment and grease the paper and the sides of the pan.

2 ▲ Add the vinegar to the milk and set aside. It will curdle.

3 In another mixing bowl, sift all the dry ingredients together three times and set aside.

4 With an electric mixer, cream the butter and sugar until light and fluffy. Beat in the egg until well combined.

5 ▼ Stir in the black treacle.

6 ▲ Fold in the dry ingredients in four batches, alternating with the milk. Mix only enough to blend.

7 Pour into the prepared tin and bake until firm, 45–50 minutes. Cut into squares and serve warm, with whipped cream. Decorate with the stem ginger.

Classic Cheesecake

SERVES 8

50g/2oz/1 cup digestive biscuits (graham crackers), crushed

900g/2lb/4 cups cream cheese, at room temperature

240g/8³/₄oz/scant 1¹/₄ cups caster (superfine) sugar

grated rind of 1 lemon

45ml/3 tbsp lemon juice

5ml/1 tsp vanilla extract

4 eggs, at room temperature

1 Preheat oven to 160°C/325°F/Gas 3. Grease a 20cm/8in springform cake tin (pan). Place on a round of foil 10–13cm/4–5in larger than the diameter of the tin. Press it up the sides to seal tightly.

2 Sprinkle the biscuits in the base of the tin. Press to form an even layer.

3 With an electric mixer, beat the cream cheese until smooth. Add the sugar, lemon rind and juice, and vanilla, and beat until blended. Beat in the eggs, one at a time. Beat just enough to blend thoroughly.

4 ▲ Pour into the prepared tin. Set the tin in a roasting pan and pour enough hot water in the roasting pan to come 2.5cm/1in up the side of the cake tin. place in the oven.

5 Bake until the top of the cake is golden brown, about 1¹/₂ hours. Leave to cool in the tin.

6 ▼ Run a knife around the edge to loosen, then remove the rim of the tin. Chill for at least 4 hours before serving.

Chocolate Cheesecake

SERVES 10–12

275g/10oz plain (semisweet) chocolate

1.2kg/2¹/₂lb/5 cups cream cheese, at room temperature

200g/7oz/1 cup caster (superfine) sugar

10ml/2 tsp vanilla extract

4 eggs, at room temperature

175ml/6fl oz/³/₄ cup sour cream

15ml/1 tbsp unsweetened cocoa powder

FOR THE BASE

200g/7oz/3¹/₂ cups chocolate biscuits (cookies), crushed

75g/3oz/6 tbsp butter, melted

2.5ml/¹/₂ tsp ground cinnamon

1 Preheat oven to 180°C/350°F/Gas 4. Grease a 23 × 7.5cm/9 × 3in springform cake tin (pan).

2 ▲ For the base, mix the biscuits with the butter and cinnamon. Press on to the base of the tin.

3 Melt the chocolate in the top of a double boiler, or in a heatproof bowl set over hot water. Set aside.

4 Beat the cream cheese until smooth, then beat in the sugar and vanilla. Add the eggs, one at a time.

5 Stir the sour cream into the cocoa powder to form a paste. Add to the cream cheese mixture. Stir in the melted chocolate.

6 ▼ Pour into the crust. Bake for 1 hour. Cool in the tin; remove the rim. Chill before serving.

Classic Cheesecake (top), Chocolate Cheesecake

Lemon Mousse Cheesecake

1.2kg/2¹/₂lb/5 cups cream cheese, at room temperature
350g/12oz/1³/₄ cups caster (superfine) sugar
40g/1¹/₂oz/¹/₃ cup plain (all-purpose) flour
4 eggs, at room temperature, separated
120ml/4fl oz/¹/₂ cup fresh lemon juice
grated rind of 2 lemons
115g/4oz/2 cups digestive biscuits (graham crackers), crushed

1 Preheat the oven to 160°C/325°F/ Gas 3. Line a 25 × 5cm/10 × 2in round cake tin (pan) with baking parchment and grease the paper.

2 With an electric mixer, beat the cream cheese until smooth. Gradually add 275g/10oz/1¹/₂ cups of the sugar, and beat until light. Beat in the flour.

3 ▲ Add the egg yolks, and lemon juice and rind, and beat until smooth and well blended.

4 In another bowl, beat the egg whites until they hold soft peaks. Add the remaining sugar and beat until stiff and glossy.

5 ▲ Add the egg whites to the cheese mixture and gently fold in.

6 Pour the mixture into the prepared tin, then place the tin in a roasting pan. Place in the oven and pour hot water in the pan to come 2.5cm/1in up the side of the tin.

7 Bake until golden, 60–65 minutes. Cool in the tin on a rack. Cover and chill for at least 4 hours.

8 To turn out, run a knife around the inside edge. Place a flat plate, bottom-side up, over the tin and invert on to the plate. Smooth the top with a metal spatula.

9 ▲ Sprinkle the biscuits over the top in an even layer, pressing down slightly to make a top crust.

10 To serve, cut slices with a sharp knife dipped in hot water.

Marbled Cheesecake

SERVES 10

50g/2oz/¹/₂ cup unsweetened cocoa powder

75ml/5 tbsp hot water

900g/2lb/4 cups cream cheese,
    at room temperature

200g/7oz/1 cup caster (superfine) sugar

4 eggs

5ml/1 tsp vanilla extract

65g/2¹/₂oz/1¹/₄ cups digestive biscuits
    (graham crackers), crushed

1 Preheat the oven to 180°C/350°F/ Gas 4. Line an 20 × 8cm/8 × 3in cake tin (pan) with baking parchment; grease.

2 Sift the cocoa powder into a bowl. Pour over the hot water and stir to dissolve. Set aside.

3 With an electric mixer, beat the cheese until smooth and creamy. Add the sugar and beat to incorporate. Beat in the eggs, one at a time. Do not overmix.

4 Divide the mixture evenly between two bowls. Stir the chocolate mixture into one, then add the vanilla to the remaining mixture.

5 ▲ Pour a cupful of the plain mixture into the centre of the tin; it will spread out into an even layer. Slowly pour over a cupful of chocolate mixture in the centre.

6 ▲ Repeat alternating cupfuls of the batters in a circular pattern until both are used up.

7 Set the tin in a roasting pan and pour in hot water to come 4cm/1¹/₂in up the sides of the cake tin.

8 Bake until the top of the cake is golden, about 1¹/₂ hours. It will rise during baking but will sink later. Leave to cool in the tin on a rack.

9 To turn out, run a knife around the inside edge. Place a flat plate, bottom-side up, over the tin and invert on to the plate.

10 ▼ Sprinkle the crushed biscuits evenly over the base, gently place another plate over them, and invert again. Cover and chill for at least 3 hours, or overnight. To serve, cut slices with a sharp knife dipped in hot water.

Heart Cake

MAKES 1 CAKE

225g/8oz/1 cup butter or margarine

225g/8oz/generous 1 cup caster (superfine) sugar

4 eggs, at room temperature

175g/6oz/1¹/₂ cups plain (all-purpose) flour

5ml/1 tsp baking powder

2.5ml/¹/₂ tsp bicarbonate of soda (baking soda)

30ml/2 tbsp milk

5ml/1 tsp vanilla extract

FOR ICING AND DECORATING

3 egg whites

350g/12oz/1³/₄ cups caster sugar

30ml/2 tbsp cold water

30ml/2 tbsp fresh lemon juice

1.5ml/¹/₄ tsp cream of tartar

pink food colouring

75–115g/3–4oz/6–8 tbsp icing (confectioners') sugar

1 Preheat the oven to 180°C/350°F/ Gas 4. Line a 20cm/8in heart-shaped tin (pan) with baking parchment; grease.

2 ▲ With an electric mixer, cream the butter or margarine and sugar until light and fluffy. Add the eggs, one at a time, beating thoroughly after each addition.

3 Sift the flour, baking powder and baking soda together. Fold the dry ingredients into the butter mixture in three batches, alternating with the milk. Stir in the vanilla.

4 ▲ Spoon the mixture into the prepared tin and bake until a skewer inserted into the centre comes out clean, 35–40 minutes. Leave the cake to stand in the tin for 5 minutes, then turn out and transfer to a rack to cool completely.

5 For the icing, combine two of the egg whites, the caster sugar, water, lemon juice and cream of tartar in the top of a double boiler or in a bowl set over simmering water. With an electric mixer, beat until thick and holding soft peaks, about 7 minutes. Remove from the heat and continue beating until the mixture is thick enough to spread. Tint the icing with the pink food colouring.

6 ▲ Put the cake on a board, about 30cm/12in square, covered in foil or in paper suitable for contact with food. Spread the icing evenly on the cake. Smooth the top and sides. Leave to set for 3–4 hours, or overnight.

7 ▲ For the paper piping (pastry) bags, fold a 28 × 20cm/11 × 8in sheet of baking parchment in half diagonally, then cut into two pieces along the fold mark. Roll over the short side, so that it meets the right-angled corner and forms a cone. To form the piping bag, hold the cone in place with one hand, wrap the point of the long side of the triangle around the cone, and tuck inside, folding over twice to secure. Snip a hole in the pointed end and slip in a small metal piping nozzle to extend about 5mm/¹/₄in.

8 For the piped decorations, place 15ml/1 tbsp of the remaining egg white in a bowl and whisk until frothy. Gradually beat in enough icing sugar to make a stiff mixture suitable for piping.

9 ▲ Spoon into a paper piping bag to half-fill. Fold over the top and squeeze to pipe decorations on the top and sides of the cake.

Forgotten Gâteau

SERVES 6

6 egg whites, at room temperature

2.5ml/^{1}/$_2$ tsp cream of tartar

pinch of salt

300g/11oz/generous 1^1/$_2$ cups caster (superfine) sugar

5ml/1 tsp vanilla extract

175ml/6fl oz/^{3}/$_4$ cup whipping cream

FOR THE SAUCE

350g/12oz/2 cups fresh or thawed frozen raspberries

30–45ml/2–3 tbsp icing (confectioners') sugar

1 Preheat the oven to 230°C/450°F/ Gas 8.

2 ▲ Grease a 1.5 litre/2^1/$_2$ pint/6^1/$_4$ cup ring mould. Beat the egg whites, cream of tartar and salt until they hold soft peaks. Add the sugar and beat until glossy and stiff. Fold in the vanilla.

3 ▲ Spoon into the prepared mould and smooth the top level.

4 Place in the oven, then turn the oven off. Leave overnight; do not open the oven door at any time.

5 ▼ To serve, gently loosen the edge with a sharp knife and turn out on to a serving plate. Whip the cream until firm. Spread it over the top and upper sides of the meringue and decorate with any meringue crumbs.

6 ▲ For the sauce, purée the fruit, then strain. Sweeten to taste. Serve with the gâteau.

~ COOK'S TIP ~

This recipe is not suitable for fan assisted and solid fuel ovens.

Iced Fancies

MAKES 16

115g/4oz/¹/₂ cup butter, at room temperature

225g/8oz/generous 1 cup caster (superfine) sugar

2 eggs, at room temperature

175g/6oz/1¹/₂ cups plain (all-purpose) flour

1.5ml/¹/₄ tsp salt

7.5ml/1¹/₂ tsp baking powder

120ml/4fl oz/¹/₂ cup plus 15ml/1 tbsp milk

5ml/1 tsp vanilla extract

FOR ICING AND DECORATING

2 large egg whites

400g/14oz/3¹/₂ cups sifted icing (confectioners') sugar

1–2 drops glycerine

juice of 1 lemon

food colourings

hundreds and thousands, for decorating

crystallized lemon and orange slices

1 Preheat oven to 190°C/375°F/Gas 5.

2 ▲ Line 16 bun-tray cups with fluted paper baking cases, or grease.

~ COOK'S TIP ~

Ready-made cake decorating products are widely available, and may be used, if you prefer, instead of the recipes given for icing and decorating. Coloured icing in ready-to-pipe tubes is useful.

3 With an electric mixer, cream the butter and sugar until light and fluffy. Add the eggs, one at a time, beating well after each addition.

4 Sift together the flour, salt and baking powder. Stir into the butter mixture, alternating with the milk. Stir in the vanilla.

5 ▲ Fill the cups half-full and bake until the tops spring back when touched lightly, about 20 minutes. Let the cakes stand in the tray for 5 minutes, then turn out and transfer to a rack to cool completely.

6 For the icing, beat the egg whites until stiff but not dry. Gradually add the sugar, glycerine and lemon juice, and continue beating for 1 minute. The consistency should be spreadable. If necessary, thin with a little water or add more sifted icing sugar to thicken.

7 ▲ Divide the icing between several bowls and tint with food colourings. Spread different coloured icings over the cooled cakes.

8 ▲ Decorate the cakes as you like, with sugar decorations such as hundreds and thousands.

9 ▲ Other decorations include crystallized orange and lemon slices. Cut into small pieces and arrange on top of the cakes. Alternatively, use other suitable sweets (candies).

10 ▲ To make freehand iced decorations, fill paper piping (pastry) bags with different coloured icings. Pipe on faces, or make other designs.

Snake Cake

SERVES 10–12

225g/8oz/1 cup butter or margarine,
    at room temperature

grated rind and juice of 1 small orange

225g/8oz/generous 1 cup caster
    (superfine) sugar

4 eggs, at room temperature, separated

175g/6oz/1½ cups plain (all-purpose) flour

5ml/1 tsp baking powder

pinch of salt

FOR THE ICING AND DECORATING

25g/1oz/2 tbsp butter, at room temperature

350g/12oz/3 cups icing (confectioners')
    sugar

150g/5oz plain (semisweet) chocolate

pinch of salt

120ml/4fl oz/½ cup sour cream

1 egg white

green and blue food colourings

1 Preheat the oven to 190°C/375°F/
Gas 5. Grease two 21cm/8½in ring
tins (pans) and dust them with flour.

2 Cream the butter or margarine,
orange rind and sugar until light.
Beat in the egg yolks, one at a time.

3 Sift the flour and baking powder.
Fold into the butter mixture,
alternating with the orange juice.

4 ▲ In another bowl, beat the egg
whites and salt until stiff.

5 Fold a large dollop of the egg
whites into the creamed butter
mixture to lighten it, then gently
fold in the remaining whites.

6 Divide the mixture between the
prepared tins and bake until a skewer
inserted into the centre comes out
clean, about 25 minutes. Leave to
stand for 5 minutes, then turn out
on to a wire rack to cool.

7 Prepare a board, 60 × 20cm/
24 × 8in, covered in paper suitable
for contact with food, or in foil.

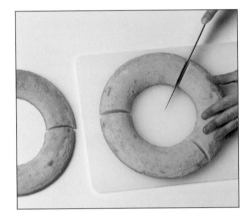

8 ▲ Cut the cakes into three even
pieces. Trim to level the flat side, if
necessary, and shape the head by
cutting off wedges from the front.
Shape the tail in the same way.

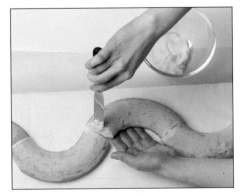

9 ▲ For the buttercream, mix the
butter with 40g/1½oz/scant ½ cup of
the icing sugar. Use to join the cake
sections and arrange on the board.

10 ▲ For the chocolate icing, melt
the chocolate. Stir in the salt and sour
cream. When cool, spread over the
cake and smooth the surface.

11 ▲ For the decoration, beat the
egg white until frothy. Add enough of
the remaining icing sugar to obtain a
thick mixture. Divide among several
bowls and add food colourings.

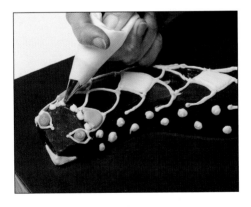

12 ▲ Fill paper piping (pastry) bags
with icing, and pipe decorations along
the top of the cake.

Sun Cake

SERVES 10–12

115g/4oz/¹/₂ cup unsalted (sweet) butter
6 eggs
225g/8oz/generous 1 cup caster (superfine) sugar
115g/4oz/1 cup plain (all-purpose) flour
2.5ml/¹/₂ tsp salt
5ml/1 tsp vanilla extract
FOR ICING AND DECORATING
25g/1oz/2 tbsp unsalted butter, at room temperature
450g/1lb/4 cups sifted icing (confectioners') sugar
120ml/4fl oz/¹/₂ cup apricot jam
30ml/2 tbsp water
2 large egg whites
1–2 drops glycerine
juice of 1 lemon
yellow and orange food colourings

1 Preheat the oven to 180°C/350°F/ Gas 4. Line two 20 × 5cm/8 × 2in round cake tins (pans), then grease and flour.

2 In a pan, melt the butter over very low heat. Skim off any foam that rises to the surface, then set aside.

3 ▲ Place a heatproof bowl over a pan of hot water. Add the eggs and sugar. Beat with an electric mixer until the mixture doubles in volume and is thick enough to leave a ribbon trail when the beaters are lifted, 8–10 minutes.

4 Sift the flour and salt together three times. Sift over the egg mixture in three batches, folding in well after each addition. Fold in the melted butter and vanilla.

5 Divide the mixture between the tins. Level the surfaces and bake until the cakes shrink slightly from the sides of the tins, 25–30 minutes. Leave to stand for 5 minutes, then turn out and transfer to a cooling rack.

6 Prepare a board, 40cm/16in square, covered in paper suitable for contact with food, or in foil.

7 ▲ For the sunbeams, cut one of the cakes into eight equal wedges. Cut away a rounded piece from the base of each so that they fit neatly up against the sides of the whole cake.

8 ▲ For the butter icing, mix the butter and 25g/1oz/¹/₄ cup of the icing sugar. Use to attach the sunbeams.

9 ▲ Melt the jam with the water and brush over the cake. Place on the board and straighten, if necessary.

10 ▲ For the icing, beat the egg whites until stiff but not dry. Gradually add 400g/14oz/3¹/₂ cups icing sugar, the glycerine and lemon juice, and continue beating for 1 minute. If necessary, thin with water or add a little more sugar. Tint with yellow food colouring and spread over the cake.

11 ▲ Divide the remaining icing in half and tint with more food colouring to obtain bright yellow and orange. Pipe decorative zigzags on the sunbeams and a face in the middle.

Jack-O'-Lantern Cake

SERVES 8–10

175g/6oz/1½ cups plain (all-purpose) flour

12.5ml/2½ tsp baking powder

pinch of salt

115g/4oz/½ cup butter,
   at room temperature

225g/8oz/generous 1 cup caster
   (superfine) sugar

3 egg yolks, at room temperature,
   well beaten

5ml/1 tsp grated lemon rind

175ml/6fl oz/¾ cup milk

FOR THE CAKE COVERING

500–675g/1¼lb–1½lb/5–6 cups icing
   (confectioners') sugar

2 egg whites

30ml/2 tbsp liquid glucose

orange and black food colourings

1 Preheat the oven to 190°C/375°F/
Gas 5. Line a 20cm/8in round cake
tin (pan) with baking parchment
and grease.

2 Sift together the flour, baking
powder and salt. Set aside.

3 With an electric mixer, cream the
butter and sugar until light and fluffy.
Gradually beat in the egg yolks, then
add the lemon rind. Fold in the flour
mixture in three batches, alternating
with the milk.

4 Spoon the mixture into the
prepared tin. Bake until a skewer
inserted into the centre comes out
clean, about 35 minutes. Leave to
stand, then turn out on to a rack.

~ COOK'S TIP ~

If you prefer, use ready-made
roll-out cake covering,
available at cake decorating
suppliers. Knead in food
colouring, if required.

5 For the icing, sift 500g/1¼lb/5 cups
of the icing sugar into a bowl. Make a
well in the centre, add 1 egg white,
the glucose and orange food
colouring. Stir until a dough forms.

6 ▲ Transfer to a clean work
surface dusted with icing sugar and
knead briefly.

7 ▲ Carefully roll out the orange
cake covering to a thin sheet.

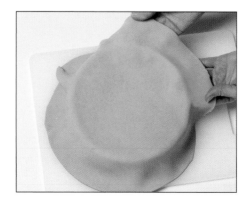

8 ▲ Place the sheet on top of the
cooled cake and smooth the sides.
Trim the excess icing and reserve.

9 ▲ From the trimmings, cut shapes
for the top. Tint the remaining cake
covering trimmings with black food
colouring. Roll out thinly and cut
shapes for the face.

10 ▲ Brush the undersides with
water and arrange the face on top
of the cake.

11 ▲ Place 15ml/1 tbsp of the
remaining egg white in a bowl and
stir in enough icing sugar to make
a thick icing. Tint with black food
colouring, fill a paper piping (pastry)
bag and complete the decoration.

Stars and Stripes Cake

SERVES 20

225g/8oz/1 cup butter or margarine, at room temperature

225g/8oz/1 cup soft dark brown sugar

225g/8oz/generous 1 cup granulated sugar

5 eggs, at room temperature

275g/10oz/2½ cups plain (all-purpose) flour

10ml/2 tsp baking powder

5ml/1 tsp bicarbonate of soda (baking soda)

5ml/1 tsp ground cinnamon

5ml/1 tsp ground ginger

2.5ml/½ tsp ground allspice

1.5ml/¼ tsp ground cloves

1.5ml/¼ tsp salt

350ml/12fl oz/1½ cups buttermilk

75g/3oz/½ cup raisins

FOR THE CAKE COVERING

25g/1oz/2 tbsp butter

1–1.25kg/2¼lb–2lb 10oz/9–10 cups icing (confectioners') sugar

3 egg whites

60ml/4 tbsp liquid glucose

red and blue food colourings

1 Preheat the oven to 180°C/350°F/ Gas 4. Line a 30 × 23cm/12 × 9in baking tin (pan) with baking parchment and lightly grease.

2 With an electric mixer, cream the butter or margarine and sugars until light and fluffy. Gradually beat in the eggs, one at a time, beating well after each addition.

3 Sift together the flour, baking powder, bicarbonate of soda, spices and salt. Fold into the butter mixture in three batches, alternating with the buttermilk. Stir in the raisins.

4 Pour the mixture into the prepared tin and bake until the cake springs back when touched lightly, about 35 minutes. Leave to stand for 10 minutes, then turn out on to a wire rack.

5 Make buttercream for assembling the cake by mixing the butter with 40g/ 1½oz/scant ½ cup of the icing sugar.

6 ▲ When the cake is cool, cut a curved shape from the top.

7 ▲ Attach it to the bottom of the cake with the buttercream.

8 Prepare a board, about 40 × 30cm/ 16 × 12in, covered in paper suitable for contact with food, or in foil. Transfer the cake to the board.

9 For the cake covering, sift 1kg/ 2¼lb/9 cups of the icing sugar into a bowl. Add two of the egg whites and the liquid glucose. Stir until the mixture forms a dough.

10 Cover and set aside half of the covering. On a clean work surface lightly dusted with icing sugar, roll out the remaining covering to a sheet. Carefully transfer to the cake. Smooth the sides and trim any excess from the bottom edges.

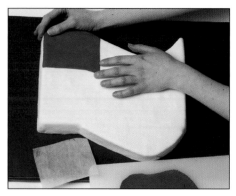

11 ▲ Tint one-quarter of the remaining covering blue and tint the remainder red. Roll out the blue to a thin sheet and cut out the background for the stars. Place on the cake.

12 ▲ Roll out the red covering, cut out stripes and place on the cake.

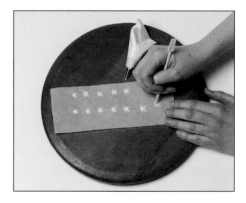

13 ▲ For the stars, mix 15ml/1 tbsp of the egg white with just enough icing sugar to thicken. Pipe small stars on to a sheet of baking parchment and leave to set. When dry, peel them off and place on the blue background.

INDEX

~